The EYES:
Am I getting it right?

Anita Soni and Su Bristow

Featherstone

Published 2010 by A&C Black Publishers Limited
36 Soho Square, London W1D 3QY
www.acblack.com

ISBN 978-1-4081-231-33

Text © Anita Soni and Sue Bristow
Design © Bob Vickers 2010

A CIP record for this publication is available from the British Library.

Printed in Great Britain by Latimer Trend & Company Ltd

This book is produced using paper that is made from wood grown in
managed, sustainable forests. It is natural, renewable and recyclable.
The logging and manufacturing processes conform to the environmental
regulations of the country of origin.

To see our full range of titles
visit www.acblack.com

Contents

Introduction and rationale

Why is self-evaluation important?

This book has been written for practitioners who work with children aged between birth and five years old, and includes those working in maintained and independent schools, in the private and voluntary sectors and childminders.

The Early Years Foundation Stage (EYFS) was implemented in all settings in England in 2008. Practitioners and their managers need to know how successful the implementation has been so far, and what still needs to be done. The EYFS documentation contains a lot of information in different formats, and can appear daunting. This book aims to help practitioners and leaders to break up the EYFS into manageable, bite-sized chunks. It provides a simple, user-friendly way of evaluating a setting against the EYFS, and assists in the long-term planning of improvement in key areas.

The book contains a framework that will enable practitioners to self-evaluate their practice and provision against the EYFS, and celebrate successes and identify priorities for improvement. This book provides the raw materials for a setting to consistently and continuously improve the standards of practice. The Effective Provision of Pre-School Education (EPPE) Project 2003 shows that higher quality provision helps children to make a good start in life.

Self-evaluation is an important part of professional development and should be undertaken regularly in all settings. Ofsted states that:

> **"Self-evaluation will help you to consider how best to create, maintain and improve your setting, so that it meets the highest standard and offers the best experience for young children."** Early Years Self-evaluation Form Guidance (Ofsted 2008, p4)

Self-evaluation enables you to look at your own development and the development of your setting, not just relying on the views and opinions of inspectors and advisers, who may not have the deep knowledge of the context of your situation. This should help reassure you and other practitioners at the setting that they are implementing the EYFS. This reassurance should lead to greater confidence when speaking to inspectors and advisers, as you will be able to explain why things are the way they are at your setting. It will also provide you with key information as you plan for development of the staff within your setting, prepare for inspections and discussions with your local authority staff team.

This book offers a self-evaluation audit will involve you in:

● reflecting on your own practice and that of others in your setting;

● considering the resources and experiences you provide for children;

● examining your indoor and outdoor environment;

● looking at the welfare requirements, the principles and the commitments, the areas of Learning and Development in the *Practice Guidance* and the relevant cards;

● planning for improvement.

What do I need for the evaluation?

There are a number of questionnaires and tools within the book which can be used for your self-evaluation audit:

- questions to support reflection on the *Statutory Framework*;
- Principles into Practice Questionnaires to identify a commitment to celebrate and the commitment to work on;
- a questionnaire for each of the 15 commitment cards (4.4 Areas of Learning and Development is incorporated in the Areas of Learning and Development Questionnaire);
- evidence collection sheets;
- Areas of Learning and Development Questionnaires to identify the areas to celebrate and those to work on;
- Key Questions sheets for three age bands (0–20 months, 16–36 months, 30–60+ months) for each of the six areas of Learning and Development. These examine the practice of the adults, knowledge of the uniqueness of the children and the environment.

Who should be involved in the evaluation?

Everyone in your setting should be involved in regular review and evaluation – practitioners, other employees, parents (although the term 'parent' is used within this book this applies to the main carers of the child while at your setting) and the children themselves. If all practitioners – full and part-time, are involved in the process, this will affect the pace and timescale of the process but makes it more effective. This book is intended for use with practitioners and parents, but views from other regular visitors such as the speech and language therapist, health visitors, and support advisers will make the information richer and more effective.

You may want to select or adapt parts of the questionnaires for some parents, and this helps to make the process your own. We have included parent versions of the Principles into Practice Questionnaire and Areas of Learning and Development Questionnaire as possible versions but you will know how to adapt them as needed, in order to suit the parents at your setting. Remember to think about the languages your parents speak and the type of words they use; this will help you to adapt the questionnaires as required.

How long will the process of evaluation take and how should it be managed?

All evaluation takes time, and this version is no exception. You can undergo the process in small sections over the course of a year, or in bigger chunks in a shorter period. If the evaluation is going to be successful, you need to allow time as you go through each stage in turn, in order that you can:

- collect information, opinions and observations;
- collate and consider these;
- decide what the information is telling you;
- identify strengths and needs;
- plan to celebrate the successes and address the needs you have identified.

You could manage this process through:

- a series of staff meetings;
- whole staff development days.

It is important to identify a person or a couple of people to coordinate the process, as they will be responsible for keeping to an agreed timetable for each of the stages above – but it is important to involve everyone!

How you undertake the process at your setting is up to you, but it is worth deciding when you are going to start the evaluation, and giving all staff notice of what is going to happen. There is a section called 'How do I use this book?' (see page 7) that gives more detailed guidance on our suggested approach, and in 'Getting started' (see page 9) there are examples of how some settings may choose to use the book, dependent on their circumstances.

What should I consider?

When completing the questionnaires remember the principles of the EYFS –

> 'Every child is a competent learner from birth who can be resilient, capable, confident and self-assured'.

Just as every child is unique so is every staff member and parent. Everyone will, therefore, complete the questionnaires differently. Some people will always underscore themselves and some people with over score. The important thing is the discussion.

> 'Children learn to be strong and independent from a base of loving and secure relationships with parents and/or a key person'

It is useful to ask both parents and/or their extended family to fill out the questionnaires as their views are just as important.

> 'The environment plays a key role in supporting and extending children's development and learning'

The environment may vary within the setting but it is important to maximise what you have got.

> 'Children develop and learn in different ways and at different rates and all areas of Learning and Development are equally important and inter-connected.'

Children are unique and will vary within each age band. The age bands on the questionnaires are broad and are to be used flexibly. There is considerable development from the beginning to the end of each age band. In this book the age bands of the EYFS have been combined from six overlapping age bands to three overlapping age bands to make it manageable for settings and practitioners.

A final point is don't be daunted by the number of questionnaires – you are not supposed to do them all in one go! Take it stage by stage and use the questionnaires as tools to support and guide you.

How do I use this book?

There are three stages to the book:

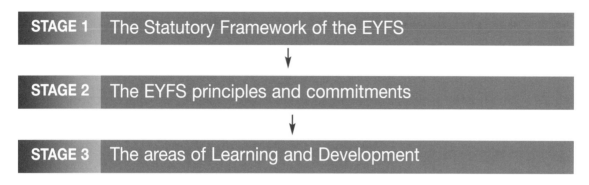

STAGE 1	The Statutory Framework of the EYFS
STAGE 2	The EYFS principles and commitments
STAGE 3	The areas of Learning and Development

Within each stage you will follow the same process as in the Early Years Quality Improvement Support Programme (National Strategies, 2008).

- **Reflect (self-evaluation audit – collect the evidence)**
- **Rate (identify and agree improvement priorities)**
- **Celebrate success**
- **Prioritise areas for development (focused improvement plan)**
- **Actions**
- **Collect evidence and celebrate (review)**

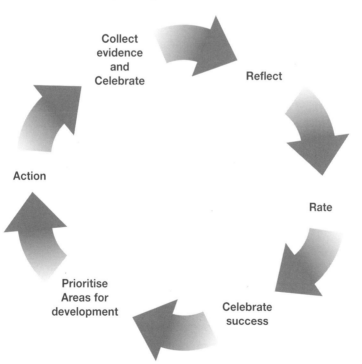

You can use this simple, step-by-step approach suggested. Alternatively you may want to evaluate a specific commitment or area of Learning and Development that you know needs work on. If this is the case you may choose to focus on a certain section of the book. It is up to you to decide what is appropriate for your setting. In writing this book we recognise that just as every child is unique, so is every setting.

The self-evaluation process

Step 1   Staff and parents complete the Principles into Practice or Areas of Learning and Development Questionnaire.

Step 2   Analyse the completed questionnaires and identify either:
- a successfully implemented commitment and a commitment to develop *or*
- an area of Learning and Development to celebrate and one to work on.

Step 3   Celebrate the successfully completed commitment or success in an area of Learning and Development.

Step 4   Reflect on the commitment to develop further by completing the appropriate Commitment questionnaire, *or*
Reflect on a second Area of Learning and Development to improve further by evaluating the appropriate Area of Learning and Development Questionnaires from Step 1. Complete Key Questions sheets.

Step 5   Begin to act upon the commitment/key questions, develop practice further, collect evidence to show this is being implemented. Use this evidence to make a display or book to demonstrate to yourself, children, parents and Ofsted that your planned actions have been successfully completed.

Step 6   Repeat the relevant steps with a different successfully implemented commitment and one to develop/areas of Learning and Developments as needed. Ensure all commitments and areas of Learning and Development are being acted upon.

Getting started

The following examples show how various settings have adopted this self-evaluation approach.

Setting A Nursery and Reception Unit within a school

Ofsted judged them 'satisfactory' with several areas identified. The team are developing their action plan and need to identify a timeline with which to achieve the actions. There is disagreement within the team about which action to start with.

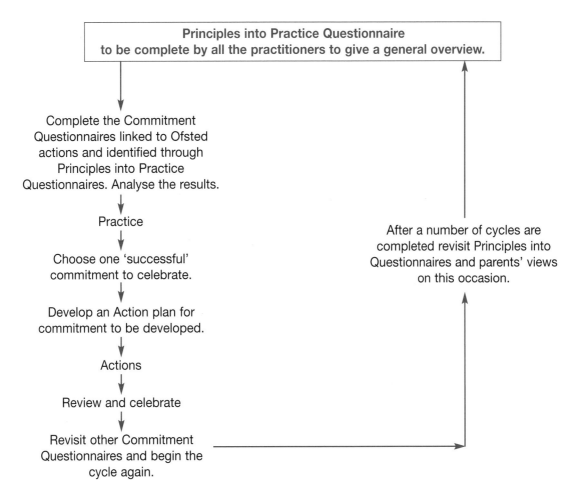

Setting B   Playgroup

OFSTED judged it 'inadequate'.

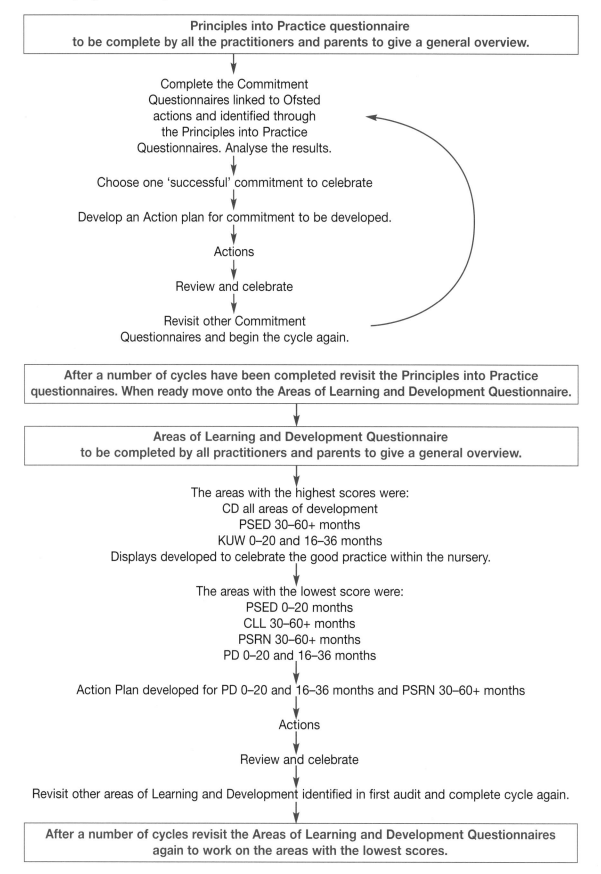

Principles into Practice questionnaire
to be complete by all the practitioners and parents to give a general overview.

Complete the Commitment
Questionnaires linked to Ofsted
actions and identified through
the Principles into Practice
Questionnaires. Analyse the results.

Choose one 'successful' commitment to celebrate

Develop an Action plan for commitment to be developed.

Actions

Review and celebrate

Revisit other Commitment
Questionnaires and begin the cycle again.

After a number of cycles have been completed revisit the Principles into Practice
questionnaires. When ready move onto the Areas of Learning and Development Questionnaire.

Areas of Learning and Development Questionnaire
to be completed by all practitioners and parents to give a general overview.

The areas with the highest scores were:
CD all areas of development
PSED 30–60+ months
KUW 0–20 and 16–36 months
Displays developed to celebrate the good practice within the nursery.

The areas with the lowest score were:
PSED 0–20 months
CLL 30–60+ months
PSRN 30–60+ months
PD 0–20 and 16–36 months

Action Plan developed for PD 0–20 and 16–36 months and PSRN 30–60+ months

Actions

Review and celebrate

Revisit other areas of Learning and Development identified in first audit and complete cycle again.

After a number of cycles revisit the Areas of Learning and Development Questionnaires
again to work on the areas with the lowest scores.

Setting C — Nursery

Ofsted judged it 'good' in all areas with a key issue regarding their key person approach. In addition there has been a change in practitioners within the toddler room and two parents have expressed concern about how unsettled their children have become.

This setting has an identified need and focus of key person and therefore does not need the Principles into Practice Questionnaires and Areas of Learning and Development Questionnaires to prioritise need. If this setting chooses, it could use the 2.4 Key Person Questionnaire alone with staff and parents to create an action plan to meet this identified need.

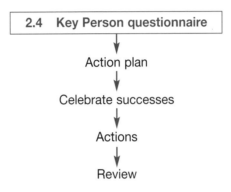

2.4   Key Person questionnaire

↓

Action plan

↓

Celebrate successes

↓

Actions

↓

Review

Setting D — Childminder

Judged 'outstanding' in all areas by Ofsted. Six months after the inspection the childminder employed an assistant to work with her who is not confident working with the six areas of Learning and Development as most of her experience has been with children aged under three.

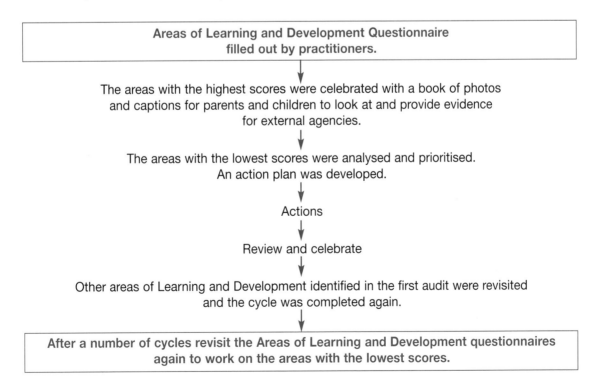

Areas of Learning and Development Questionnaire
filled out by practitioners.

↓

The areas with the highest scores were celebrated with a book of photos
and captions for parents and children to look at and provide evidence
for external agencies.

↓

The areas with the lowest scores were analysed and prioritised.
An action plan was developed.

↓

Actions

↓

Review and celebrate

↓

Other areas of Learning and Development identified in the first audit were revisited
and the cycle was completed again.

↓

After a number of cycles revisit the Areas of Learning and Development questionnaires
again to work on the areas with the lowest scores.

Collecting evidence

It is important to have evidence to show what you have done and are doing. However evidence can come in many forms, not just paper and it is important to remember this at all times.

What is evidence?

Evidence can be:

- displays on the wall;

- your planning;

- comments, notes and cards from parents;

- how you interact and behave with the children;

- children's comments;

- photographs of the children, environment;

- learning and development records or journals;

- questionnaires by staff, parents or visitors;

- visit notes from outside agencies such as local authority development officers, speech and language therapists, college placement supervisors and so on;

- documentation such as policies and procedures;

- reflections on your own practice;

- observations;

- children's work.

The Statutory Framework
of the EYFS

This is the best place to start to have a quick check to ensure you are meeting the statutory requirements of the EYFS, before moving on to the rest of the book and further evaluating the quality at your setting.

The EYFS is given legal force through an Order and Regulations made under the Childcare Act 2006. It is mandatory for all Schools and Early Years Providers in Ofsted registered settings attended by young children – children from birth to the end of the academic year in which a child has their fifth birthday.

The *Statutory Framework for the Early Years Foundation Stage* sets out:
- legal requirements related to learning and development;
- legal requirements relating to welfare.

The learning and development requirements are given legal force by the Early Years Foundation Stage (Learning and Development Requirements) Order 2007 made under Section 39 (1) (a) of the Childcare Act 2006. The welfare requirements are given legal force by Regulations made under Section 39 (1) (b) of the Childcare Act 2006. The requirements have statutory force by virtue of Section 44 (1) of the Childcare Act 2006.

In order to help consider the legal requirements of the *Statutory Framework*, these have been listed in the following pages, alongside some prompt questions. However it is important to read the full *Statutory Framework* for guidance and clarification on all points.

The EYFS Learning and Development requirements:

Learning and Development requirements	Questions to support
The Early Learning Goals – the knowledge, skills and understanding which young children should have acquired by the end of the academic year in which they reach five. The Early Learning Goals establish the expectations for most children to reach by the end of the EYFS.	Do you plan and organise your setting to support the children achieving the Early Learning Goals by the end of their Reception year? Do you use the Early Learning Goals and development matters statements to inform and support your planning for the children in the setting? See the *Statutory Framework for the EYFS* for full details on the Early Learning Goals.
The educational programmes – the matters, skills and processes which are required to be taught to young children. None of these areas of Learning and Development can be delivered in isolation from the others. They are equally important and depend on each other to support a rounded approach to child development. All the areas must be delivered through planned, purposeful play, with a balance of adult-led and child-initiated activities.	Do you consider the educational programmes for the six areas of Learning and Development when planning opportunities for the children in the setting? The educational programme for each area of Learning and Development is also shown on each of the six areas of Learning and Development cards. See the *Statutory Framework for the EYFS* for full details on the educational programme.
The assessment arrangements – the arrangements for assessing young children to ascertain their achievements. Providers must ensure that practitioners are observing children and responding appropriately to help them make progress from birth towards the Early Learning Goals. Assessments should be based on practitioners' observation of what children are doing in their day-to-day activities.	Do you observe the children and respond to them appropriately to help them progress towards the Early Learning Goals? Are your assessments based on your observations of what you see and hear children doing in their day-to-day activities? Do you use the Early Learning Goals and development matters statements to support your observation and assessment processes? Do your assessments take account of information provided by parents? See the *Statutory Framework for the EYFS* for full details on the assessment arrangements.

The EYFS Welfare requirements:

Welfare requirements	Questions to support
Safeguarding and promoting children's welfare The provider must take necessary steps to safeguard and promote the welfare of children.	Do you have an effective safeguarding children policy and procedures and meet all the specific legal requirements? Do you engage with parents and provide them with and obtain the necessary information? Are the premises, outdoor and indoor, safe and secure? Are children kept safe on outings? Do you have an effective policy about ensuring equality of opportunity for all children?
The provider must promote the good health of the children, take necessary steps to prevent the spread of infection, and take appropriate action when they are ill.	Do you have an effective policy on administering medicines? Do you meet the specific legal requirements for illnesses and injuries? Do you meet the specific legal requirements for food and drink? Do you ensure that the children are in a smoke-free environment?
Children's behaviour must be managed effectively and in a manner appropriate for their stage of development and particular individual needs.	Do you have an effective behaviour management policy? See the *Statutory Framework for the EYFS* (pages 22–28) for full details on the Safeguarding and promoting children's welfare.
Suitable people Providers must ensure that adults looking after children, or having unsupervised access to them, are suitable to do so.	Do you follow the specific guidance on safe recruitment given in the *Statutory Framework for the EYFS*? Do you notify Ofsted as required about relevant changes to staff?
Adults looking after children must have appropriate qualifications, training, skills and knowledge.	Do staff in the settings have the appropriate qualifications?
Staffing arrangements must be organised to ensure safety and to meet the needs of children.	Are the minimum adult-child ratios as defined in the *Statutory Framework for the EYFS*? See the *Statutory Framework for the EYFS* (pages 29-32) for full details on Suitable People.
Suitable premises, environment and equipment Outdoor and indoor spaces, furniture, equipment and toys must be safe and suitable for their purpose.	Are risk assessments conducted and hazards to children, indoor and outdoor, kept to a minimum? Are the premises maintained to ensure the safety of children, staff and others in the setting? Are the premises and equipment organised in a way to meet the needs of the children? See the *Statutory Framework for the EYFS* (pages 33-36) for full details on Suitable premises, environment and equipment.

The EYFS Welfare requirements (continued):

Welfare requirements	Questions to support
Organisation Providers must plan and organise their systems to ensure that every child receives an enjoyable and challenging learning and development experience that is tailored to meet their individual needs.	Are effective systems in place to ensure that the needs of every child are met? See the *Statutory Framework for the EYFS* (page 37) for full details on Organisation.
Documentation Providers must maintain records, policies and procedures required for the safe and efficient management of the settings and to meet the needs of the children.	Is the data kept as is required in the specific legal requirements? Are the records and documentation kept as required in the specific legal requirements? See the *Statutory Framework for the EYFS* (page 38) for full details on the Documentation.

It is important that the setting meets these legal requirements (Early Years Officers will be able to advise and support on this if needed), once you have considered these questions; you are ready to move on to the next step, **Step 2 The Principles into Practice questionnaire.**

STAGE 2

The EYFS principles and commitments

The 'Principles into Practice' cards form the basis of the EYFS and this is, therefore, the place to move on to after considering the *Statutory Framework*. The principles and commitments need to be implemented consistently to promote effective practice and quality within your setting. For your self-evaluation use the step-by-step approach outlined below.

STEP 1 Staff and parents to complete the Principles into Practice Questionnaire.

The Principles into Practice card is a very important tool to use in evaluating your setting. It is a useful card to plan longer term priorities for the setting.

There are two versions of the Principles into Practice Questionnaire:
- one presents each commitment as a statement and then phrased as a question (for staff, see pages 22–23).
- one presents each commitment as a question (for parents, see page 24).

It is up to you which version you choose to use and photocopy. Choose the one that best suits the staff and parents at your setting.

Photocopy one questionnaire per staff member/parent. Ask each staff member and parent to rank how well they feel the setting is doing on each commitment by using a simple scale below:

1	2	3	4	5

Just starting work on this commitment · · · Fully implementing this commitment

When self-evaluating it is important to emphasise that high marks are not the order of the day but that it is important that everyone is honest about the practice in the setting and is willing and open to reflect on change. It is easier to complete this questionnaire quickly and not spend too long on considering each commitment in great depth as this is meant as a quick overview, and there is opportunity for detailed discussion later.

Compile the questionnaire results in the table on page 25. Write the scores (1, 2, 3, 4, 5) in the third and fourth columns for each person who has completed the questionnaire and then total them in the final column of the table.

Card number	Commitment	Scores		Total
		Practitioner's	Parent's	
1.1	Child Development			
1.2	Inclusive Practice			
1.3	Keeping Safe			
1.4	Health and Well-being			
2.1	Respecting Each Other			
2.2	Parents as Partners			
2.3	Supporting Learning			
2.4	Key Person			
3.1	Observation, Assessment and Planning			
3.2	Supporting Every Child			
3.3	The Learning Environment			
3.4	The Wider Context			
4.1	Play and exploration			
4.2	Active Learning			
4.3	Creativity and Critical Thinking			

STEP 2   Analyse the completed questionnaires and identify a successfully implemented commitment and a commitment to develop.

Look carefully at the results of your completed questionnaires. The commitments with the highest score are those that everyone feels the setting is doing very well, those with lower scores are the ones which would benefit from further development.

Once you have chosen the commitment that requires some attention, reflect on this commitment by asking staff at the setting to complete a copy of the appropriate Commitment Questionnaire (see pages 28–42). To develop practice further it is important to answer the questions honestly and to be able to prove which areas of the commitment are being already covered by filling in the evidence sheet (see page 00). The collated evidence sheets from all the staff will show the effective practice in place already and where the evidence is available but also will indicate where the evidence is required.

For example, for the question 'How do you support children's transitions between key person relationships in the setting when there are staff changes?' (see 2.4 Key Person, page 35) Possible evidence might be:

- the new key person visits the child in the room;
- parents are invited in to be introduced to the new key person and to visit the new room;
- transition form on the child is filled in and passed on;
- the child visits the new key person and room.

Lack of evidence for the question will require staff to discuss this further and agree any actions that need to take place. See page 27 for an example of a completed evidence sheet.

STEP 3   Celebrate the successfully completed commitment.

Choose the highest scoring commitment. This is one that the setting is doing well, and celebrate! Make a display or book to demonstrate to yourself, children, parents and Ofsted that you are already doing this part of the EYFS well. The display or book should contain a variety of evidence including photographs, comments from parents and children, planning and children's work. This is important! It might be tempting to overlook those commitments that the setting is implementing successfully, but celebrating good practice is vital for the morale of staff, parents and children.

STEP 4   Reflect on the commitment to develop further by completing the appropriate Commitment Questionnaire.

Choose the commitment that scores the lowest, this is the commitment that requires some attention. Reflect on this commitment by asking everyone to complete a copy of the appropriate photocopiable Commitment Questionnaire (see pages 28–42). The completed questionnaires and evidence sheets will show which parts of this commitment the setting needs to develop further.

STEP 5   Begin to act upon the Commitment Questionnaire, develop practice further, collect evidence to show this is being implemented.

Analyse the responses to the questionnaires, and use this information to develop your practice. A photocopiable Action Plan can be found on page 43. Collect evidence to show that the resulting actions taken have been successful. Use this evidence to make a display or book to demonstrate to yourself, the children, parents and Ofsted that your planned actions have been successfully completed. Ideas for development of practice can come from a number of sources including discussion and reflection with other practitioners, the relevant EYFS commitment card and additional information on the EYFS CD-ROM.

STEP 6   Repeat the relevant steps with a different, successfully implemented commitment and a commitment to develop, as needed.

This cycle needs to be repeated until you as a setting feel comfortable with the commitments. This can be reviewed by completing Step 1 again if you want. Ensure that all commitments are being acted upon.

STAGE 3

The areas of Learning and Development

Once your setting has reflected upon the Principles into Practice card, and the commitments within it, the next stage is to consider the areas of Learning and Development. This is the 16th commitment and needs reflecting upon in the same way as the other 15 commitments. However there is much more to consider within this commitment as there are links to the remaining six areas of Learning and Development cards and the *Practice Guidance for the EYFS*. To begin to evaluate your practice within the Areas of Learning and Development follow the step-by-step approach below.

STEP 1 All staff (and possibly parents) to complete the Areas of Learning and Development Questionnaire.

The questionnaire is presented using the educational programmes described in the *Statutory Framework* for the EYFS. There are two versions, one for practitioners and one for parents:

● The questionnaire for practitioners provides a statement about each area of Learning and Development and a question for practitioners to consider (see page 44). They should rank how well they feel the setting is doing on each area of Learning and Development by using the simple scale below:

1	2	3	4	5

Just starting work on this area
of Learning and Development

Fully implementing this area
of Learning and Development

Ask staff to consider this in relation to which of the following three broad age bands they are working with: 0–20 months; 16–36 months; 30–60+ months.

● The questionnaire for parents provides simple questions about the educational programme for each Area of Learning and Development (see pages 45–46). They can rate how well they think the setting is doing by ticking various aspects of the curriculum.

When self-evaluating it will be important to emphasise that high marks are not the order of the day but that it is important that everyone is honest about the practice in the setting and is willing and open to reflect on change. It is easier to complete this quickly and not spend too long on considering each section in great depth as this is meant as a quick overview, and there is opportunity for detailed discussion later.

Photocopy one questionnaire per staff member/parent. Ask each person to fill in a questionnaire and then compile the results in the following table (see page 47). Write the scores (1, 2, 3, 4, 5) in the third column for each person who has completed the questionnaire and then total them in the final column of the table.

Area of Learning and Development	Scores			Total
	0–20 months	16–36 months	30–60+ months	
Personal, Social and Emotional Development				
Communication, Language and Literacy				
Problem Solving, Reasoning and Numeracy				
Knowledge and Understanding of the World				
Physical Development				
Creative Development				
Learning and Development				

STEP 2   Analyse the completed questionnaires and identify an area of Learning and Development to celebrate and one to work on.

We suggest, initially, identifying two out of the six areas of Learning and Development:

- one that is a strength for the setting and should be celebrated;
- one that requires some work.

This is done by totalling the scores each area of Learning and Development has been given by each person and then seeing which area has come top with the highest score, and which has come at the bottom with the lowest score.

The area of Learning and Development with the highest score is the one everyone feels is being implemented most confidently; the one with the lowest score is the one that people understand the least or feel least confident with.

This may vary from age band to age band. It may be that in your setting the staff in the baby room (working with children aged 0–20 months) are unsure of Problem Solving, Reasoning and Numeracy but for pre-school (30–60+ months) Personal, Social and Emotional Development is an area to consider. Therefore the area of Learning and Development that you choose to focus on needs to come from your analysis. Alternatively if your setting only covers one age band (30–60+ months) you need only focus on this.

STEP 3   Celebrate success in an area of Learning and Development.

Choose the highest scoring area of Learning and Development. This is one that the setting is doing well so celebrate! Make a display or book to demonstrate to yourself, children, parents and Ofsted that you are already doing this part of the EYFS well. This is important! It might be tempting to overlook those areas of Learning and Development that the setting is implementing successfully, but celebrating good practice is vital for the morale and confidence of staff, parents and children.

STEP 4   Reflect on a second area of Learning and Development to improve further by evaluating the appropriate area of Learning and Development questionnaires from Step 1. Complete Key Questions sheets.

Choose the area of Learning and Development that scores the lowest; this is the one that requires some attention. Reflect on this area of Learning and Development by asking everyone to now complete the more detailed Key Questions photocopiable sheets (see pages 48–104) which focus on specific aspects of the areas of Learning and Development. There are three sheets for each area of Learning and Development, covering the three age bands:

- 0–20 months
- 16–36 months
- 30–60+ months

The sheets consider practice related to the EYFS themes:

- A Unique Child
- Positive Relationships
- Enabling Environments.

The Key Questions for each area of Learning and Development cover the following format. This example is for Personal, Social and Emotional Development:

- **Let's look at the Personal, Social and Emotional Development of your unique key children.**
  This sheet helps you to check that you know all about the Personal, Social and Emotional development of each of your key children.

  It will need to be photocopied for each key child and should be completed by the key person. It is designed as a quick questionnaire to help you identify the aspects of your key child that you know a lot about, and aspects that you may want to know more about. Observations of your key child, talking to other staff and talking to your key child's parents may be a helpful way of finding out any missing information.

- **How do the adults support the Personal, Social and Emotional Development of their key children?**
  This sheet is to be filled in by each key person. You need to think about the children in your key group when looking at the bank of questions and then rate your practice from 1–5 for an overall score for each bank of questions.

  It may lead you to reflect on all the effective practice you already have, and also to find out more about certain key children or an aspect of their days and lives. It may be that you want to do more to promote their Personal, Social and Emotional Development. The *Practice Guidance for the EYFS* has lots of useful ideas for effective practice to help you with this.

- **Resources and experiences that promote Personal, Social and Emotional Development (PSED)**
  This sheet helps you to think about your environment and whether you have the resources and experiences to promote Personal, Social and Emotional Development. Score your environment from 1–5, and then you may find some ideas on how to develop your environment further in the *Practice Guidance for the EYFS* and the Enabling Environment cards..

STEP 5 Begin to act upon the Key Questions results, develop practice further, collect evidence to show how this is being implemented.

Analyse the responses in the Key Questions, develop practice further by looking at the gaps identified by staff within the questionnaires and decide on actions to fill the gaps identified. A photocopiable Action Plan can be found on page 43. As actions are completed collect the evidence to show that the actions taken have been successful so that a display or book can be developed to celebrate the improvements made. This can be shared with staff, children, parents and Ofsted.

STEP 6 Repeat the relevant steps with a different successfully implemented area of Learning and Development and one to develop as needed. Ensure all areas of Learning and Development are being acted upon.

Ideas for development of practice can come from a number of sources including discussion with other practitioners and reflection; the relevant area of Learning and Development in the *Practice Guidance for the EYFS* (in particular the column identifying Effective practice); the relevant area of Learning and Development card and information contained on the CD-ROM.

Rate how well each commitment is being achieved in the setting from 1 to 5.

1	2	3	4	5
Just starting work on this commitment				Fully implementing this commitment

Card number	Title of commitment	Commitment	Question	Rating (1–5)
1.1	Child Development	Babies and young children develop in individual ways and at varying rates. Every area of development – physical, cognitive, linguistic, spiritual, social and emotional – is equally important.	Are the babies and young children allowed to develop in individual ways and at varying rates? Is every area of development – physical, cognitive, linguistic, spiritual, social and emotional – treated as equally important?	
1.2	Inclusive Practice	The diversity of individuals and communities is valued and respected. No child or family is discriminated against.	Is the diversity of individuals and communities valued and respected? Are any children or families discriminated against?	
1.3	Keeping Safe	Young children are vulnerable. They develop resilience when their physical and psychological well-being is protected by adults.	Are young children recognised as vulnerable? Is young children's physical and psychological well-being protected by adults in order that they can develop resilience?	
1.4	Health and Well-being	Children's health is an integral part of their emotional, mental, social, environmental and spiritual well-being and is supported by attention to these aspects.	Are all aspects of children's health – emotional, mental, social, environmental and spiritual recognised and supported by giving attention to these aspects?	
2.1	Respecting Each Other	Every interaction is based on caring professional relationships and respectful acknowledgement of the feelings of children and their families.	Is every interaction based on caring professional relationships and respectful acknowledgement of the feelings of children and their families?	
2.2	Parents as Partners	Parents are children's first and most enduring educators. When parents and practitioners work together in early years settings, the results have a positive impact on children's development and learning.	Are parents recognised as their child's first and most enduring educators? Do parents and practitioners work together in relation to the children's development and learning in the setting?	
2.3	Supporting Learning	Warm, trusting relationships with knowledgeable adults support children's learning more effectively than any amount of resources.	Are there warm, trusting relationships between knowledgeable adults and the children to support the children's learning?	
2.4	Key Person	A key person has special responsibilities for working with a small number of children, giving them the reassurance to feel safe and cared for and building relationships with their parents.	Is there a key person system in the setting where each key person has special responsibilities for working with a small number of children, giving them the reassurance to feel safe and cared for and building relationships with their parents?	

continued on next sheet

Rate how well each commitment is being achieved in the setting from 1 to 5.

1	2	3	4	5
Just starting work on this commitment				Fully implementing this commitment

Card number	Title of commitment	Commitment	Question	Rating (1–5)
3.1	Observation, Assessment and Planning	Babies and young children are individuals first, each with a unique profile of abilities. Schedules and routines should flow with the child's needs. All planning starts with observing children in order to understand and consider their current interests, development and learning.	Are babies and young children recognised as individuals with a unique profile of abilities? Do schedules and routines flow with the child's needs? Does the planning start with observing children and their current interests, development and learning?	
3.2	Supporting Every Child	The environment supports every child's learning through planned experiences and activities that are challenging but achievable	Does the setting's environment support every child's learning through planned experiences and activities that are challenging but achievable?	
3.3	The Learning Environment	A rich and varied environment supports children's learning and development. It gives them the confidence to explore and learn in secure and safe, yet challenging, indoor and outdoor spaces.	Has the setting got a rich and varied environment that supports children's learning and development and gives them the confidence to explore and learn in secure and safe, yet challenging, indoor and outdoor spaces?	
3.4	The Wider Context	Working in partnership with other settings, other professionals and with individuals and groups in the community supports children's development and progress towards the outcomes of *Every Child Matters*: being healthy, staying safe, enjoying and achieving, making a positive contribution and economic well-being.	Does the setting work in partnership with other settings, other professionals and with individuals and groups in the community supporting children's development and progress towards the outcomes of *Every Child Matters*: being healthy, staying safe, enjoying and achieving, making a positive contribution and economic well-being?	
4.1	Play and exploration	Children's play reflects their wide ranging and varied interests and preoccupations. In their play children learn at their highest level. Play with peers is important for children's development.	Does children's play reflect their wide ranging and varied interests and preoccupations and allow children to learn at their highest level? Is play with peers taking place?	
4.2	Active Learning	Children learn best through physical and mental challenges. Active learning involves other people, objects, ideas and events that engage and involve children for sustained periods.	Do children have opportunities for active learning that involves other people, objects, ideas and events that engage and involve children for sustained periods?	
4.3	Creativity and Critical Thinking	When children have opportunities to play with ideas in different situations and with a variety of resources, they discover connections and come to new and better understandings and ways of doing things. Adult support in this process enhances their ability to think critically and ask questions.	Do children have opportunities to play with ideas in different situations and with a variety of resources so they discover connections and come to new and better understandings and ways of doing things? Do adults supporting this process enhance children's ability to think critically and ask questions?	

Your name (optional): _____   Child's name (optional): _____

Rate how well each commitment is being achieved in the setting from 1 to 5 for your child.

1	2	3	4	5

Just starting to do this   Fully doing this

Card number	Title of commitment	Question on the commitment	Rating (1–5)
1.1	Child Development	Is your child allowed to develop fully in their own way at their own rate?	
1.2	Inclusive Practice	Is your child, family and community valued and respected rather than discriminated against?	
1.3	Keeping Safe	Is your child kept safe, physically and emotionally, and protected by adults?	
1.4	Health and Well-being	Is your child's health and well-being recognised and supported by the adults in the setting?	
2.1	Respecting Each Other	Do the adults in the setting respect you, your family and your child and your feelings?	
2.2	Parents as Partners	Do the adults in the setting recognise you as your child's first and most important teacher?	
2.3	Supporting Learning	Are there warm, trusting relationships between the adults in the setting and the children? Do you think the adults are knowledgeable about your child and their job?	
2.4	Key Person	Is there someone in the setting who works to build relationships with your child and you?	
3.1	Observation, Assessment and Planning	Do the setting's ideas and activities recognise that your child is an individual with their particular interests?	
3.2	Supporting Every Child	Does the setting support your child's learning with experiences and activities that are challenging but achievable?	
3.3	The Learning Environment	Is the setting secure, safe and challenging to support your child's learning and development, both indoor and outdoor?	
3.4	The Wider Context	Does the setting work with other settings, other professionals and with individuals and groups in the community?	
4.1	Play and exploration	Can the children play with friends and toys or objects that interest them?	
4.2	Active Learning	Does your child have opportunities to actively learn, doing things that engage and sustain him/her?	
4.3	Creativity and Critical Thinking	Do adults help your child to play with ideas and resources in different situations to discover connections and understand different ways of doing things?	

Card number	Commitment	Scores		Total
		Practitioner's	Parent's	
1.1	Child Development			
1.2	Inclusive Practice			
1.3	Keeping Safe			
1.4	Health and Well-being			
2.1	Respecting Each Other			
2.2	Parents as Partners			
2.3	Supporting Learning			
2.4	Key Person			
3.1	Observation, Assessment and Planning			
3.2	Supporting Every Child			
3.3	The Learning Environment			
3.4	The Wider Context			
4.1	Play and Exploration			
4.2	Active Learning			
4.3	Creativity and Critical Thinking			

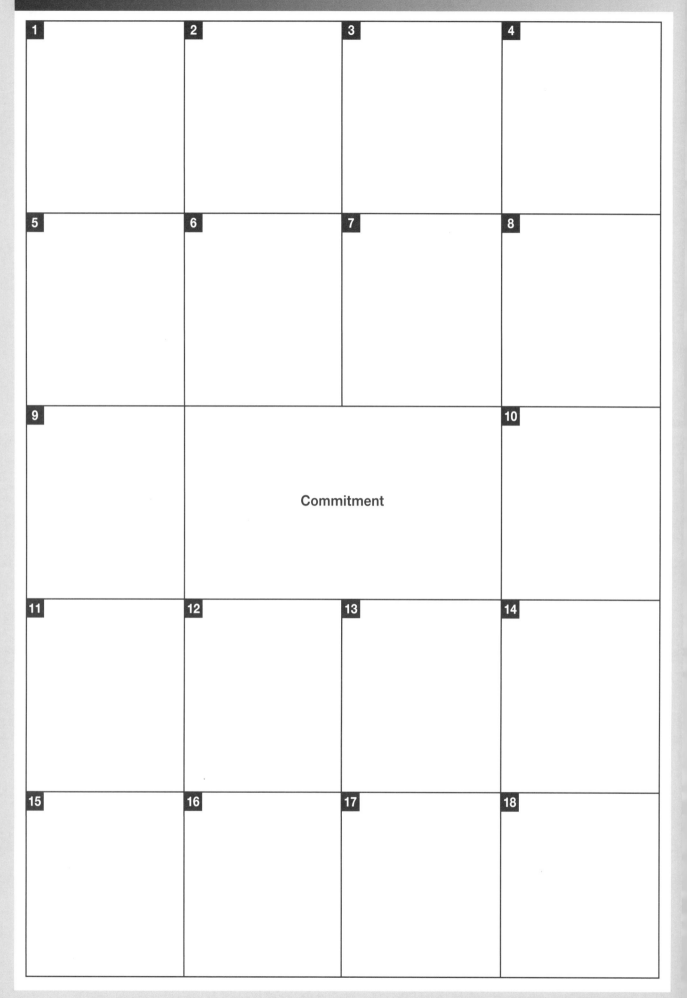

Commitment

1

Visit at home.
Detailed induction information.
Key person gets to know the family during induction.
Key person and 'Buddy' available at both ends of the day.
Key person biographies displayed.

2

Induction and moving rooms is planned at the child's pace.
Pictures of the child's family displayed in the environment.
Each child has a 'tray' for their personal things.
Minor changes are made to the room arrangement throughout the year.

3

Learning journeys are sent home every three months and parents are asked to add their observations and photographs.
Key person shares the learning journey with each key child and the child has an opportunity to add their favourite photographs and work to them.
A speech and language therapist visited a child in the room and his learning journey was shared with her.

4

Informal discussions with the staff in the room about how to support the new experience with each child.
Key person to support the new experience if possible.
Talk to child about experience beforehand and parent if necessary.

5

Jake likes to be cuddled when sad.
Shivani likes to be with best friend Anna.

6

Informal support from room leader.
Regular supervision.

7

Display on the key person role in the entrance.
Training for staff on the key person role.

8

Daily home and nursery communication book.
Three-monthly meetings.

9

Key person or buddy always available where possible.
Transitional objects welcomed from home as well as nursery.
See Transition form for movement between rooms.
See Room handbooks given when each child moves room.
Staff given time to move up with them and help the child make a relationship with their new key person.

A key person has special responsibilities for working with a small number of children, giving them the reassurance to feel safe and cared for and building relationships with their parents.

10

Key person training for all staff identified in key person policy.
Staff support each other as necessary.

11

Each child has a key person and a back up key person called a 'buddy'. Rotas are planned so that where possible either staff member is available at all times.

12

See question 11.

13

Where possible the 'buddy' takes on the primary key person role and the new member of staff becomes the 'buddy'.

14

See question 11

15

Pictures of the child's family displayed in the environment.
Each child has a 'tray' for their personal things.
Cosy area is available in the room.
Resources that children recognise from home and are interested in are available in the room.

16

On the agenda for next staff meeting.

17

Home and nursery communication book.
Regular newsletters, email and texts.
Staff phone parents every three months.

18

Observe children to see how staff can plan to support 'friendships'.
Friendships are shared with parents so that parents can make links outside of nursery.
Senior management plan to spend time in rooms.
The cook visits the children every week to plan the menus.
Parents are invited in to spend time in the nursery and share their skills, such as cooking.

1
Does your planning show that you start from activities relating to what children can do? Give examples.

2
How well do you know each child's characteristics and temperament? Think of each of your key children in turn. Where is this shown?

3
How do you know you allow the children to explore the resources and environment in their own way? For example, photographs of the environment.

4
How do you show you recognise how important practitioners are for the children?

5
How do you show you know the important details about each child in your key group? For example, planning; special interest sheets.

6
Do you communicate, play and spend time with all your key children every time they come to your setting? Think of each of your key children in turn.

7
Do you allow the children to communicate in many different ways by using their talk, gaze, drawing, writing, singing, dancing, music and drama? Consider evidence for verbal and non-verbal communication.

8
Do you let children do the activities and experiences rather than tell them or show them? Give an example.

9
Do you know about each of your key children's culture and background? Where does this show in the setting?

Babies and children develop in individual ways and at varying rates. Every area of development – physical, cognitive, linguistic, spiritual, social and emotional, is equally important.

10
Where do your records show that you know what each child is interested in and what makes them smile?

11
How do you let children learn and develop at their own pace and not rush them or slow them down? Give examples.

12
Do you recognise and praise children for effort as well as achievement? Give examples.

13
When do you listen and respond to verbal and non-verbal communication from the babies and children? Give examples.

14
How do you make sure that you spend time with every child 'fairly'?

15
Where in your planning and records do you show recognition of all areas of development?

16
Do you allow children to say what they want/need to say, no matter how long it takes? Give an example.

17
Where in your planning of activities and experiences are each child's interests represented?

18
How does your setting show it has a key person system for each child and his/her parents?

1 Do you smile, welcome and listen to all the families? Think of each of your families in your key group in turn.

2 Where do you show that you include children from socially excluded families such as the homeless, or those who live with a parent who is disabled or has a mental illness? For example, display?

3 Where do you show that you include children from traveller communities, refugees, asylum seekers and those from diverse linguistic backgrounds? For example, policy?

4 Where do you show that you include children who are disabled and those who have special educational needs? For example, play resources?

5 How do you keep your knowledge about religions and different cultural groups up to date?

6 How do you allow children to develop as individuals with their own cultural and spiritual beliefs?

7 When do you reflect on your attitudes to people who are different to you?

8 When do you ask parents whether any specialist services or equipment is needed for children who need additional support?

9 Do you treat all children fairly regardless of their race, religion, abilities, what they think or do, the languages they speak, what their parents do and whether they have a disability or their social background? Where is this recorded?

The diversity of individuals and communities is valued and respected. No child or family is discriminated against.

10 How do you take part in sensitive two-way exchange of information with all families?

11 How do you listen to all children and show that you value what they have to say?

12 How do you ensure you identify children who need additional support as early as possible so that they can get the help they need?

13 Do you have records that are suitable for sharing with other agencies, for example, health visitors, speech and language therapists?

14 Do you have displays, objects and photographs that relate to the families who use the setting?

15 Do you plan jointly with everyone who is in contact with children who have severe and complex support needs, for example, families and other professionals? Where is this recorded?

16 Do you know when and how to call in specialist support for children and families? How would you find out?

17 How do you encourage children to recognise their own unique qualities and the characteristics they share with other children? For example, displays?

18 Where do your displays and photographs show the names of the staff and welcome children from a variety of cultures and languages?

1
Where are the clear limits on what children may and may not do recorded, for example, signs, policy? Are they reinforced consistently by all practitioners?

2
Do you explain the rules, boundaries and limits to the children in a way that they can understand? Give an example.

3
How do you encourage children to contribute to deciding what are the limits, rules and boundaries so they understand them?

4
How do you work with parents to have consistent boundaries for behaviour at home and in the setting?

5
How do you keep an open and flexible dialogue with parents and professionals whose views about child-rearing or behaviour are different to yours?

6
What stories do you read about everyday events so children know who to trust and how to keep safe? When do you talk about this?

7
How do you help children to assertively say no when needed?

8
Do you listen to what children tell you and act on non-verbal signals especially from children who are anxious? Give examples.

9
Do you let children choose not to join in even if they are the only one to do so? Give an example.

Young children are vulnerable. They develop resilience when their physical and psychological well-being is protected by adults.

10
Do you explain to the children why they are allowed to choose and times when they are not allowed? Give examples of how you give children choices so they learn to choose and help themselves?

11
How do you encourage children to make choices over what they wear or do, to give them some sense of control?

12
When do you let children do things for themselves and still give an appropriate level of support where needed?

13
Do you encourage, listen and respond to verbal and non-verbal communication from the babies and children? Give examples.

14
What activities and experiences do you give that help children know how to recognise and avoid possible danger and think about ways to keep safe?

15
What activities and experiences do you provide that help children feel good about themselves?

16
What activities and experiences for the children are about people who help them?

17
When do you let children have time to think about what they want and express that rather than making decisions for them?

18
When do you help and show children how you assess the risks in the setting?

The EYFS: Am I getting it right? © Anita Soni & Sue Bristow

1
How do you ensure the children are safe without stopping reasonable risk taking?

2
How do you encourage the children to move around the room to different activities and resources as they play?

3
How do you help children to understand why some choices in food and drink are healthier than others?

4
Do you know how to recognise child abuse and neglect? Who do you consult if there is a cause for concern?

5
Do you plan that babies and children with special needs access similar opportunities to their peers? Give an example.

6
Do all the children have a close relationship with their key person? How do you do this? Is this reviewed regularly?

7
Are the children encouraged to join in and help with manageable tasks around the setting? Give an example.

8
How do you encourage parents and grandparents to share their knowledge of their child with you?

9
How do you create relationships with the children that are close, warm and supportive?

Children's health is an integral part of their emotional, mental, social, environmental and spiritual well-being and is supported by attention to these aspects.

10
When do the children have access to the outdoors?

11
What is in place to ensure the environment is clean and safe?

12
How well do you know the care routines for feeding, toileting and sleeping for each individual child? Think of each of your key children in turn.

13
Do you present food and items from other cultures as an every day experience within the setting not as a novelty? Give an example.

14
How do you encourage the children to make friends and play with each other?

15
Is there a balance of activities so children can be involved, and rest and relax at different times? Where are the places for children to sleep, rest or relax?

16
How are the parents involved in promoting their child's health and well-being in the setting? Are their photographs displayed or are they asked to bring in resources?

17
How do you help children know about the food chain? Do you plant, grow and use the foods grown with the children?

18
Where are the large, interesting spaces for energetic movement indoors and outdoors?

1 How do you show that you recognise the feelings of the adults and children in the setting?

2 How do you show that you respect and value the strengths, skills and knowledge of the people that you work with?

3 How is each child, parent and practitioner valued for who they are and their differences appreciated?

4 How do you support the children in making friends with each other?

5 How do you support the children who are shy or find it difficult to interact or to make friends?

6 How do you help children who find it difficult to get on and play with others and be friendly?

7 How do you ensure you work in partnership with parents and are friendly but maintain a professional distance?

8 When do you recognise and label the feelings expressed by the children, including those that can be more challenging like anger?

9 When do you allow the children to practically help and emotionally support each other?

Every interaction is based on caring professional relationships and respectful acknowledgement of the feelings of children and their families.

10 How are the contributions of each person recognised in your setting?

11 In your setting, how do you show you make best use of the people available to best meet the needs of the children?

12 How do you deal with strong feelings or personal prejudices about an issue that may be a barrier to supporting a child and their family?

13 How does communication at the setting include everyone's views while keeping the needs of the children firmly in mind?

14 When do you listen to parents' feelings, concerns and views?

15 Are you aware that different factors will affect children's and families' ability to be friendly?

16 How does the setting support mutual respect between staff members themselves?

17 How does the setting support mutual respect between parents and children?

18 How does the setting support mutual respect between staff and children?

1 How do you ensure all families are welcomed and valued in your setting?

2 How do you greet children and parents in the setting? Are these greetings used at home by families in your setting?

3 Do you show recognition of the different types of families in your displays, books, photographs, posters? Give examples.

4 How do you create an atmosphere at the setting that allows communication between parents and the setting?

5 Give examples of the two-way flow of information, knowledge and expertise between parents and practitioners?

6 How do you support parents in understanding more about learning and teaching on areas such as play, outdoor learning, early reading and so on?

7 How do you give opportunities for parents to review their child's progress regularly and contribute to their child's learning and development record?

8 How do you show you value the different home languages used by children in the setting?

9 When and how do you create opportunities for informal talk with parents?

Parents are children's first and most enduring educators. When parents and practitioners work together in early years settings, the results have a positive impact on children's development and learning.

10 When do you involve parents in writing words from their home language, for example, to use in displays, books and so on?

11 As a staff member, when do you talk about diversity, equality and anti-oppressive practice?

12 How do you seek the views of parents on the care and education provided in the setting?

13 How can the parents of the children communicate with the setting, for example, daily books?

14 Give examples of the way your setting 'communicates' with parents who are busy or working.

15 How does the setting recognise and value the role played by parents in developing their child's learning and development?

16 How do you ensure the parents understand and contribute to the setting's policies in key areas such as learning and teaching, inclusion and behaviour?

17 Do you run/signpost family learning courses and other opportunities for parents to access learning?

18 How do you get fathers and male family members involved in the setting?

1
What does each child like to do?
When is each child confident, scared or frustrated?
Think of each key child in turn.

2
How do you use your observations to encourage and extend the children's learning?

3
How do you motivate and encourage children to persist and try several ways to make things work rather than giving up at the first attempt?

4
What do you do to ensure that children are given time and space to respond?

5
How do you build respectful, caring relationships with all the children and families while focusing on learning and achievement?

6
How do you ensure you listen to babies and younger children who have a delay in their speech or who speak English as an additional language?

7
Give examples of different ways you help the children make connections in their learning.

8
When do you model being a learner with the children, for example, by talking about the problem and asking the children to help solve it?

9
How do you encourage children to reflect on their learning?

Warm, trusting relationships with knowledgeable adults support children's learning more effectively than any amount of resources.

10
What examples can you give of following the children's lead in play?

11
How do you help each child to know you are genuinely pleased to see them each day?

12
How do you make sure activities, stories and play experiences are pitched at the right level for each child?

13
When have you listened to and acted on children's views that don't match your own? Give examples.

14
Who are the children you find more difficult to build positive relationships with and how could you get to know them better?

15
How do you help the children feel confident to try new things and take on challenges?

16
How do you ensure that you intervene in children's learning at the right time rather than dominate it?

17
How often do you record yourself in a group activity, and then reflect on who talks the most and what sort of talk it is?

18
Give examples of when you actively listen and respond to children.

1 In what ways do you build a genuine bond with each child and their family?

2 How do you help your key children become familiar with the environment and feel safe in it?

3 How do you ensure that each key child's records of progress and development are created and shared by parents, the child, the key person and other professionals?

4 How do you support the children in exploring new experiences and activities?

5 How do you ensure you respond sensitively to each of your key children's feelings, ideas and behaviour?
Consider each of your key children in turn.

6 What support is available for practitioners who start to feel too attached to a key child?

7 How do you reassure staff and parents that children will not become too dependent on their key person?

8 Do you talk to parents of your key children regularly so you know how to care for them? How often does this happen?

9 How do you support children and parents in transitions? Are they given time with and information about their new key person when they move rooms or settings?

A key person has special responsibilities for working with a small number of children, giving them the reassurance to feel safe and cared for and building relationships with their parents.

10 Do you recognise that children and babies are likely to be less independent when in new situations or when unwell or anxious? How do you support this?

11 How do you ensure that each child can be reassured and comforted by key adults at times they may need it?

12 Who is the key person for each child? When does the key person 'spend' time with each key child?

13 How do you support children's transitions between key person relationships in the setting when there are staff changes?

14 Who is the back-up key person for each child for when the key person is away for breaks, courses, holiday and so on?

15 How do you help the setting feel familiar and comfortable for each child especially any new ones?

16 Do you reflect on how your setting might feel to different parents and children?
How is this achieved?

17 How do you communicate with parents of your key children who are very busy and don't have time to talk?

18 How do you support children to make relationships with other children and other adults?

1 Do you know what each child needs, is interested in and can do?
Think of each of your key children in turn.

2 How does your planning show how you support each child's learning and development?

3 What do you know about the Common Assessment Framework (CAF) for children with additional needs so you can be involved as needed?
Are there any areas you would like further explanation of?

4 When do you analyse your observations to consider who needs more support and who has achieved something new?
Do you do this alone or in conjunction with others?

5 Where are the assessments of children's learning and development and can the children and parents access them?

6 Are your records clear and accessible for everybody who wants to see them including the child and parents?

7 How do you ensure that parents have regular opportunities to add to their child's learning and development record?

8 How do you involve parents in the ongoing observation and assessment process?

9 Where are the views of the parents shown in the children's records?

Babies and young children are individuals first, each with a unique profile of abilities. Schedules and routines should flow with the child's needs. All planning starts with observing children in order to understand and consider their current interests, development and learning.

10 How do you involve busy or working parents in observing and planning for their children?

11 Do you observe children in different situations and at different times of their day?

12 How do you ensure you observe children who attend the setting on an irregular basis?

13 Is your planning flexible so the children can learn from spontaneous events such as a fall of snow?

14 How does your planning reflect each of your child's interests?
Think of each of your key children in turn.

15 How do you ensure you observe as a part of the daily routine?

16 How do you show the ideas on your planning come from observing the children and analysing these observations?

17 How and when do you review a child's level of involvement in different activities to help you plan?

18 Do you review your environment and resources during or after each session as part of your planning?

The EYFS: Am I getting it right? © Anita Soni & Sue Bristow

1 How do you know when to support children and when to step back?

2 How do you make sure you follow every child's individual interests and needs in their learning?

3 How do you ensure you give some new and interesting challenges?

4 How do you ensure that you offer a range of experiences to the children, including some that are comforting, familiar and predictable?

5 How do you ensure that the children are always able to have their physical needs met? Consider their needs for food, water, sleep and rest?

6 How do you work with the child's parents to achieve the best for each child?

7 How do you ensure you listen to children's needs in the learning process?

8 How do you involve people from the wider community in children's learning?

9 How do you communicate with other settings a child may go to at the same time, or have been to or will go to?

The environment supports every child's learning through planned experiences and activities that are challenging but achievable.

10 How can you make the most ordinary events such as going to the toilet, setting the table and getting ready to go home, more exciting and interesting for the children?

11 Can you give examples of how you provide appropriate, realistic experiences that build on children's interests?

12 Can you give examples of how you bring children's experiences of home into the learning?

13 How do you keep your planning for individual children realistic while keeping a focus on broader learning outcomes in the *Practice Guidance*?

14 Give examples of how you have extended a child's special talents and things they are good at.

15 How do you ensure that the children are always able to have their emotional needs met? Consider the need for a hug, encouragement or reassurance.

16 How does the setting make sure that what is written in a policy happens in reality day-to-day?

17 How do you work with other professionals who may be involved with one of your key children to achieve the best for this child?

18 How do you involve the children in making choices about planned experiences and activities?

1 How do you create a warm and accepting emotional environment at the setting?

2 How do you show you empathise with the children and encourage them all to express their emotions?

3 How do you create an indoor environment that is reassuring and comforting for the children but still provide interest and novelty?

4 How do you show the children that you accept all their emotions not just happiness and joy?

5 What support is there for practitioners who may feel drained when a child requires high levels of support for their strong feelings of sadness, anger or frustration?

6 How do you ensure that you allow children to have first-hand contact with different weathers and seasons and aspects of the natural world?

7 How do you involve children in planning the layout of the room so they are more likely to respect it and keep it tidy?

8 How do you give children the best opportunity to learn outdoors on a daily basis as well as indoors?

9 How do you promote the importance and value of outdoor play to all those involved in the setting including parents and staff?

**A rich and varied environment supports children's learning and development.
It gives them confidence to explore and learn in secure and safe, yet challenging, indoor and outdoor spaces.**

10 How do you help children to understand how to behave outdoors and inside?

11 How do you encourage the children to experience learning both inside and outside?

12 How well do you reflect examples of outdoor learning as well as indoor learning in your observations and assessments?

13 How do you ensure deployment of staff is flexible enough to respond to the flow and movement of children between indoors and outdoors?

14 How do you encourage the children to link indoor and outdoor environments?

15 How do you show you value children's efforts rather than just their achievements and products?

16 How do you adapt and plan your indoor environment and spaces to make best use of them and provide a range of activities?

17 How do you develop the indoor environment to be 'homely' for the children but still promote learning?

18 How do you ensure your resources are appropriate, well maintained and accessible for the children?

1 How do you effectively communicate with any other settings each child attends?

2 How do you effectively communicate with previous settings the child has attended or a future setting?

3 How do you share the children's records of development and learning with other settings the child may attend?

4 How do you support children and parents with transition times, for example, start/end of day and changes of rooms, especially those who find it stressful?

5 How do you show you value what parents tell you about their child on induction?

6 How do you involve parents in transition times such as induction and settling in times and in other decisions about their child?

7 How do you keep parents informed in advance of what will happen at transition times such as when children join the setting?

8 Do you have a policy for transition shared with everyone involved in and beyond the setting?

9 How do you help children and families who are new to the area or your setting to settle in and get to know people?

Working in partnership with other settings, other professionals and with individuals and groups in the community supports children's development and progress towards the outcomes of *Every Child Matters*: being healthy, staying safe, enjoying and achieving, making a positive contribution and economic well-being.

10 How do you ensure you put the child's needs first when you work with other agencies, for example, health visitors, speech therapists?

11 What other agencies do you work with to help children achieve the *Every Child Matters* outcomes: being healthy; staying safe; enjoying and achieving; making a positive contribution and achieving economic well-being?

12 How do ensure you value and respect colleagues from other professional backgrounds?

13 How do you make your records of children's learning and development accessible and easy to share with other agencies?

14 How do you use the local community to support the children's learning?

15 How do you and the setting work and make links with other early years provision in the local community?

16 How do you get members of the local community to share their expertise, for example, gardening, storytelling and get involved in the setting?

17 How do you and the setting show you value the local community?

18 How well do you and other staff know the local area and how much do you use this knowledge in planning for children's learning?

1 Where can children choose to play alone in the setting?

2 Where can children play with other children? How do you encourage children to play either in parallel or together?

3 Where can children role play and act out things they may be worried about like monsters, new babies, the doctors?

4 Do children get the chance to play indoors and outdoors every day? How often?

5 Do you let children play where they can solve problems, take risks and find things out themselves? Give an example.

6 Can the children play with resources and equipment before trying to solve a problem with them? Give an example.

7 How do you develop children's language and communication when playing with them?

8 When do you plan activities for children to play with in their own way, where the end result may be different for every child? Give an example from your planning.

9 Can the children make dens and play dressing-up?

Children's play reflects their wide ranging and varied interests and preoccupations. In their play children learn at their highest level. Play with peers is important for children's development.

10 When have you told or read stories for children to act out themselves?

11 Where can the children access role-play resources of their choice?

12 Do you challenge any play that is racist, sexist, offensive, unsafe or violent? Give an example.

13 When have you allowed play based on superheroes and other ideas that mean a lot to children even if they don't mean much to you?

14 Do you observe and watch before deciding to join in with children's play? Give an example.

15 What flexible resources do you have that can be used in many different ways? For example, fabric and pegs, boxes, clothes horses, blankets and tablecloths?

16 How are the parents involved in the setting and the children's play? Do you have parents' photographs up? Or do you ask them to bring in resources?

17 Do you base play on themes that the children may like even if you don't? Give an example.

18 How do you know how children like to play at home?

1 Are all the children at ease, secure and confident? How do you know?

2 When do you challenge and extend the children's thinking? Give an example.

3 Do you know the activities each child gets mostly involved in? Think of each key child in turn.

4 When do you find out from parents what activities and play their child gets most involved with at home?

5 How do you let children control and make decisions about their play and learning? When do children make choices about what they use, and how it looks at the end?

6 How are the children's learning journeys shared with the child, their parents and peers? For example, through displays, records, and photographs?

7 How and when do you review your environment to ensure it is interesting, accessible and attractive to every child within it?

8 How do you promote children investigating and exploring new ideas for themselves?

9 How do you ensure every child's learning journey is unique from other children's?

Children learn best through physical and mental challenges. Active learning involves other people, objects, ideas and events that engage and involve children for sustained periods.

10 When do you encourage the children to ask questions?

11 How do you make sure that your expectations are realistic for each child?

12 Where does your planning reflect the interests and learning of each child?

13 When do you analyse and reflect on what has been observed to show what children have learned?

14 Do the children have time, space and independence in their own learning to follow their own ideas and what they are interested in? Where and when?

15 How do you consider how long children are involved in their learning and use this information in planning? Give an example from planning.

16 How do you keep the learning active for each child?

17 When do you look at the nature and quality of adult interactions in children's learning? For example, evaluations?

18 How do you show that your planning comes from your observations and information from talking to the child and from their parents?

1
How do you show that you value children's home lives/culture? Do you let them share items from home?

2
How do you develop individual creativity in children? Give an example of an open-ended activity.

3
How do you help children make connections between experiences? When do they have opportunities to repeat experiences in different ways?

4
How do you recognise the process of being creative? For example, through recording observations or by taking photographs of the process?

5
When do you let children play with the process, for example, glue and paper, before expecting them to make products like cards?

6
When and how do you show genuine interest in, encourage and clarify children's ideas to support their thinking?

7
Do you model being creative in your thinking of ideas and making creative items? Give an example.

8
How do you share the observations and photographs with the children? When do you re-visit learning and reflect on the child's thinking?

9
How do you know what each child is interested in and understands? How do you work with this information to develop them further?

When children have opportunities to play with ideas in different situations and with a variety of resources, they discover connections and come to new and better understandings and ways of doing things. Adult support in this process enhances their ability to think critically and ask questions.

10
How do you support and challenge children's thinking and ideas? Have you ever taped your interactions with children to see how you support their development of creativity and critical thinking?

11
Where do you record how children's thinking develops? When do you share the photographs and observations with parents?

12
How do you find out about and value children's learning and behaviour from their parents? How do you find out how they behave at home and support this?

13
How do you ensure that you have a balance of adult-led and child-initiated activities?

14
Do you allow the children to take things from one area to another, indoor and outdoor, so they can make connections? Give an example. At the same time how do you ensure they understand the importance of looking after their things and tidying up?

15
What kind of open questions do you ask? Give an example.

16
When do you let children express their ideas in different ways: movement, dance, drawing and writing. How do you show that you value each one equally?

17
When can children choose to repeat activities and experiences as many times as they want? Give an example.

18
When can children produce their own creation rather than everyone's being the same?

Early Years Foundation Stage focus _____

e.g. area of Learning and Development or commitment

What are you going to do?	How are you going to do it?	Who?	When?	Resources?	How will you know when this action has been achieved?

Circle age group working with: 0–20 months   16–36 months   30–60 +months

Rate the setting on how far you have got with each area of Learning and Development:

1	2	3	4	5

Just starting work on this area
of Learning and Development

Fully implementing this area
of Learning and Development

Area of Learning and Development	Rating (1–5)

Personal, Social and Emotional Development
Children must be provided with experiences and support which will help them to develop a positive sense of themselves and of others; respect for others; social skills; and a positive disposition to learn. Providers must ensure support for children's emotional well-being to help them to know themselves and what they can do.
How much do the experiences and support given to the children help them feel positive about themselves, recognise what they can do, respect others, develop social skills and feel positive about learning?

Communication, Language and Literacy
Children's learning and competence in communicating, speaking and listening, being read to and beginning to read and write must be supported and extended. They must be provided with opportunity and encouragement to use their skills in a range of situations and for a range of purposes, and be supported in developing the confidence and disposition to do so.
How varied and positive are the experiences and opportunities given to children help them to develop skills in communicating, speaking and listening, reading and writing? How much are children encouraged to feel good about using these skills?

Problem solving, Reasoning and Numeracy
Children must be supported in developing their understanding of Problem solving, Reasoning and Numeracy in a broad range of contexts in which they can explore, enjoy, learn, practise and talk about their developing understanding. They must be provided with opportunities to practise and extend their skills in these areas and to gain confidence and competence in their use.
How much do the experiences allow children to explore, enjoy, learn, practise and talk about their understanding of problem solving, reasoning and numeracy? How are children encouraged to feel confident about these skills?

Knowledge and Understanding of the World
Children must be supported in developing the knowledge, skills and understanding that help them make sense of the world. Their learning must be supported through offering opportunities for them to use a range of tools safely; encounter creatures, people, plants and objects in their natural environments and in real-life situations; undertake practical 'experiments'; and work with a range of materials.
How much do the opportunities given to children allow them to develop their knowledge, skills and understanding of the world? How much do children get to come across a range of creatures, people, plants and objects, undertake practical learning and work with a range of materials?

Physical Development
The physical development of babies and young children must be encouraged through the provision of opportunities for them to be active and interactive and to improve their skills of coordination, control, manipulation and movement. They must be supported in using all of their senses to learn about the world around them and to make connections between new information and what they already know. They must be supported in developing an understanding of the importance of physical activity and making healthy choices in relation to food.
How much do the experiences offered help the children to develop skills of coordination, control, manipulation and movement? How much are the children helped to use their senses to learn about the world, to understand the importance of physical activity and healthy food?

Creative Development
Children's creativity must be extended by the provision of support for their curiosity, exploration and play. They must be provided with opportunities to explore and share their thoughts, ideas and feelings, for example, through a variety of art, music, movement, dance, imaginative and role-play activities, mathematics, and design and technology.
How much are children encouraged to be curious, explore and play, share their ideas and feelings in a variety of art, music, movement, dance, imaginative and role-play activities, mathematics, design and technology?

Learning and Development
The six areas of Learning and Development are presented as separate areas but it is important to remember that for children everything links and nothing is compartmentalised.
The challenge for practitioners is to ensure that children's learning and development occur as an outcome of their individual interests and abilities and that planning for learning and development takes account of these.
How linked up is the learning for children? How much of the children's learning and development is planned to come from their individual interests and abilities?

Please rate how well the setting is doing on each area of Learning and Development by ticking whether you feel each section is being covered:

Area of Learning and Development	Total out of 5

Personal, Social and Emotional Development

Is your child offered varied and positive experiences to help them develop in the following:

1. feeling good about himself or herself
2. respect for others
3. social skills
4. positive attitude to learning
5. feeling good about what he/she can do?

Any comments on your child's Personal, Social and Emotional Development?

Communication, Language and Literacy

Is your child offered varied and positive experiences to help them develop in the following:

1. communicating
2. speaking and listening
3. reading
4. writing
5. feeling good about using these skills?

Any comments on your child's Communication, Language and Literacy Development?

Problem Solving, Reasoning and Numeracy

Do the experiences offered help your child to develop:

1. talk
2. explore problem solving
3. learn to reason
4. enjoy and practise using numbers
5. feel confident about these skills?

Any comments on your child's development of Problem Solving, Reasoning and Numeracy?

Knowledge and Understanding of the World

How much do the opportunities given to children allow them to:

1. develop their knowledge, skills and understanding of the world
2. come across a range of creatures and plants
3. come across a range of people and objects
4. undertake practical learning
5. work with a range of materials?

Any comments on your child's development of Knowledge and Understanding of the World?

Please rate how well the setting is doing on each area of Learning and Development by ticking whether you feel each section is being covered:

Area of Learning and Development	Total out of 5

Physical Development
Do the experiences offered help your child to develop:
1. skills in coordination
2. control
3. manipulation and movement
4. use their senses to learn about the world
5. an understanding of the importance of physical activity and healthy food?

Any comments on your child's Physical Development?

Knowledge and Understanding of the World
How much do the opportunities given to children allow them to:
1. develop their knowledge, skills and understanding of the world
2. come across a range of creatures and plants
3. come across a range of people and objects
4. undertake practical learning
5. work with a range of materials?

Any comments on your child's development of Knowledge and Understanding of the World?

Physical Development
Do the experiences offered help your child to develop:
1. skills in coordination
2. control
3. manipulation and movement
4. use their senses to learn about the world
5. an understanding of the importance of physical activity and healthy food?

Any comments on your child's Physical Development?

Creative Development
How much is your child encouraged to:
1. be curious
2. explore mathematics
3. share their ideas and feelings in a variety of art, music, movement, dance activities
4. take part in imaginative and role play activities
5. explore design and technology?

Any comment on your child's Creative Development?

Learning and Development
How much of your child's learning and development is planned from their individual interests and abilities?

1	2	3	4	5
A tiny bit				All of it!

Total score out of 30

Area of Learning and Development	Scores			Total
	0–20 months	16–36 months	30–60+ months	
Personal, Social and Emotional Development				
Communication, Language and Literacy				
Problem Solving, Reasoning and Numeracy				
Knowledge and Understanding of the World				
Physical Development				
Creative Development				
Learning and Development				

Personal, Social and Emotional Development

Let's look at the Personal, Social and Emotional Development of your unique key children.

Read the following questions and think about each key child in your group as you read each one. Remember the many ways babies communicate and respond by eye-contact, grasping, head-turning, wiggling toes, smiling, banging, vocalising and facial expressions.

How much do you know about _____ (key child's name)?

- How this baby moves and explores the environment?
- How this baby communicates their dislikes and likes?
- How this baby responds to other adults and children?
- How this baby plays with their feet, hands and toys placed near them?
- How this baby responds when content and their needs have been met?
- How this baby shows feelings of excitement, anger, fear and frustration?
- How long this baby can play independently and when this happens?
- Who this baby likes to be with (adults and children)?
- How this baby responds to you when you give them attention?
- How this baby makes contact and communicates with others?
- What soothes and relaxes this baby?
- What toys, books or experiences does this baby prefer?
- How this baby responds to praise for doing what you say?
- How this baby shows hunger and responds to food?
- How this baby shows what they want?
- How this baby show pleasure or interest?
- How this baby responds when they know you have heard them?

Is there a particular aspect of this baby that you know less about?

How will you get this information? Through observations of the baby, talking to other staff or parents?

How do the adults support the Personal, Social and Emotional Development of their key children?

Think about all the babies in your key group, and give yourself an overall score for each section on the scale below:

Do you?

- Sing rhymes/songs to each baby encouraging them to join in by pointing to their hands/feet?
- Playfully help each baby recognise they are different from others by pointing to own and babies' nose/eyes and fingers?
- Give each baby a choice where possible?
- Have uninterrupted, individual time with each baby to build a secure relationship?
- Follow each baby's lead as they explore the surroundings, people and resources?
- Respond to each baby's actions, expressions and gestures?
- Actively listen and give full attention to each baby when they communicate by mirroring movements and vocalisations?
- Ensure you greet and say goodbye to each baby as you arrive or leave or as the baby leaves or arrives?
- Have conversations with every baby?
- Greet and say goodbye to each baby's parents at the beginning and end of each session?
- Respond to what each baby shows they are interested in?
- Imitate each baby playfully and interact with them on their own terms?
- Talk to each baby about the people and places they know?
- Talk to each baby as they play near you to show you are there and interested in them?

1	2	3	4	5

Just beginning to...   Doing it all!

Do you discuss with parents (using support/translation as needed):

- Their baby's development and progress?
- Their baby's likes and dislikes?
- How to respond to their baby's cries and emotions to develop a shared understanding of how to respond?
- How their baby communicates its needs?
- Their baby's cultural and feeding needs?
- The boundaries that are in place at the setting and at home to create consistency for the baby?
- The routine each baby has at home?
- The songs and lullabies sung at home so that you can sing them at the setting?

1	2	3	4	5

Just beginning to...   Doing it all!

Who do you need to know more about?

Is there a particular aspect of the babies' day and lives that you want to develop?

Resources and experiences that promote Personal, Social and Emotional Development.

Think about your environment. Do you have:

- Mirrors to help the babies explore what they look like?
- A choice of different vegetables and fruit at snack time?
- Enough space for the babies to roll, move, stretch and explore?
- Foods and cultural artefacts that reflect the babies' lives at home?
- Different languages displayed in the baby room?
- Records of the home languages of the babies that are shared with other staff?
- Accessible toys and comforters for the babies that are easy to locate?
- Areas for the babies to be able to snuggle into staff?
- Resources such as picture books and stories that reflect different emotions, for example, I am happy books?
- Times when the babies and older siblings/friends can be together?
- Special toys for the babies to hold while you prepare food or get materials for a nappy change?
- A comfy chair or sofa so parents, practitioners and the babies can sit together?
- Gentle music to play to the babies when they are tired?
- Cosy places with views for the babies to see what is happening beyond their room?
- A variety of games, activities and stories that build on the babies' interests?
- A place to talk quietly to the babies indoors and out?
- Photographs of each baby's family, pets and homes that they can see and talk about them?

Rate your environment from 1–5

1	2	3	4	5

Just beginning to enable   Very enabling environment

How could you improve your environment and make it even more enabling for Personal, Social and Emotional Development?

Let's look at the Personal, Social and Emotional Development of your unique key children.

Read the following questions and think about each key child in your group as you read each one.

How much do you know about _____ (key child's name)?

Dispositions and Attitudes

- The activities this key child is likely to play with independently?
- What this key child is confident to have a go at?
- Who (child or adult) this key child prefers?
- This key child's special skills and qualities?

Self-confidence and Self-esteem

- The challenges this key child will set himself, for example, climbing on a chair?
- Whether this key child can pour their drink, feed themselves and make choices?
- How this key child shows their feelings of anger, enthusiasm, fear, anxiety?

Making Relationships

- Who this key child plays with or tends to avoid?
- Whether this key child looks at their key person to check what they are doing is ok?
- How this key child shows concern for others?

Behaviour and Self-control

- Whether this key child knows what is theirs or belongs to others, for example, cups, comforters?
- How this key child responds when someone is hurt or could be harmed?
- How this key child responds to stories about others who may be hurt or harmed?

Self-care

- The feeding and changing routines of this key child?
- Whether this key child can take off or put on their own clothes?
- What this key child chooses to play with or do?

Sense of Community

- This key child's family, culture, religion, home and life beyond the setting?

Is there a particular aspect of this key child that you know less about?

How will you get this information? Through observations of the key child, talking to other staff or parents?

How do the adults support the Personal, Social and Emotional Development of their key children?

Think about all the children in your key group, and give yourself an overall score for each section on the scale below:

Do you?

- Ensure each child is recognised as a valuable contributor to the group?
- Celebrate each child's cultural, religious and ethnic experiences?
- Know each child's interests and preferences and how they vary?
- Build on your knowledge of how each child responds to activities, adults and their peers to plan future activities and experiences?
- Allow each child with disabilities to make choices?
- Recognise the possible dangers while balancing the importance of each child exploring?
- Involve every child in welcoming and caring for each other?
- Praise and recognise in your words and actions, the effort each child has made?
- Evaluate how you respond to every child?
- Give your full attention when each child looks to you for a response?
- Help each child label their feelings by talking about them?
- Help each child join in, by talking about rules such as waiting for a turn?
- Keep routines flexible to reduce each child's frustrations?
- Help each child understand their right to be safe?
- Encourage each child to talk about ways of avoiding hurting others?
- Allow time for each child to complete a self-chosen task such as putting their shoes on independently?
- Support each child's growing independence, for example, encourage them to try to pull up their own pants after the toilet?
- Talk to each child about their choices and help them understand if they can't have their preferred choice?
- Help each child learn each other's names through songs and rhymes?
- Help each child accept difference in others and be aware that negative attitudes to difference come from what children see?
- Talk to each child about their friends and families and why they're important?

1	2	3	4	5

Just beginning to...   Doing it all!

Do you discuss with parents (using support/translation as needed):

- How their child responds to activities, adults and their peers?
- Their child's concerns so you know how and when to reassure their child?
- Your policies and practice to ensure a two-way dialogue about them?
- Their child's independence as there can be variation in attitudes to children developing independence?

1	2	3	4	5

Just beginning to...   Doing it all!

Who do you need to know more about?

Is there a particular aspect of the children's day and lives that you want to develop?

Resources and experiences that promote Personal, Social and Emotional Development.

Think about your environment. Do you have:

- Resources that reflect the diversity of the children and adults within and beyond the setting?
- A display of photographs of the staff so parents can show their children who is looking after them today?
- Individual records of achievement that reflect significant progress for every child?
- Resources for pretend play so the children can express feelings through role play?
- Books and stories in which characters show empathy for others?
- Books and stories that have characters that are going through a significant transition, for example, starting a new setting, moving house?
- Books showing a wide variety of backgrounds that avoid negative stereotypes?
- Photograph books and stories about the children in the setting, with parents encouraged to contribute?
- Areas where the children can sit and chat together, for example, a snug den?
- Duplicate resources to reduce conflict, for example, two copies of a popular book?
- Agreed procedures on how to respond to changes in the children's behaviour?
- The children pouring their own drinks, serving their own food, watering the plants?
- Stories showing the consequences of actions for the characters?
- Pictures and objects to help the children make and express their choices?
- Pictures of groups of the children showing what they look like, like to do, eat and play with?
- Positive images of all the children including those with disabilities?
- Dolls and puppets to help you tell stories about diverse experiences and help children develop empathy?
- Photographs of the children's families, friends, pets or favourite people?

Rate your environment from 1–5

1	2	3	4	5

Just beginning to enable   Very enabling environment

How could you improve your environment and make it even more enabling for Personal, Social and Emotional Development?

Personal, Social and Emotional Development

Personal, Social and Emotional Development

Let's look at the Personal, Social and Emotional Development of your unique key children.

Read the following questions and think about each key child in your group as you read each one.

How much do you know about _____ (key child's name)?

Dispositions and Attitudes

- What activities is this key child confident to have a go at or wary of?
- Which activities absorb this key child?
- Which situations is this key child likely to be confident and independent in?
- How does this key child respond to a new activity (excited, worried, happy)?
- Who are the adults and children this key child likes to be with?
- How does this key child respond to adults and children they like?
- Can this key child talk and listen to others at group time and in play?

Self-confidence and Self-esteem

- How does this key child express their needs?
- Is this key child able to talk about their home/community with pride?
- How does this key child express their different feelings?
- How does this key child feel about themselves and what they can do?
- How sensitive is this key child to the views, needs and feelings of others?
- How does this key child feel about their own culture and beliefs and those of others?

Making Relationships

- How does this key child show they like to be cared for and kept safe?
- Does this key child like to be with other children or needs support to join in?
- How does this key child respond to change?
- Can this key child wait for their turn?
- How does this key child share ideas with others, for example, introduces new ideas to play, lead play?
- Who are the special people in this key child's life?

Behaviour and Self-control

- How does this key child recognise the needs of others?
- How does this key child show care for the others and the environment?
- How does this key child show they understand the boundaries at their setting?
- Does this key child understand how they should behave and how others should behave to them?
- What does this key child recognise as right and wrong and why?
- Is this key child aware of the consequences of their words and actions?

Self-care

- How does this key child celebrate their success?
- How does this key child set about an activity?
- Can this key child recognise and manage their own needs (coat, drink, rest)?

Sense of Community

- Can this key child draw upon experiences beyond the setting, for example, 'You're like my gran!'?
- Can this key child respect and show interest in different ways of life?
- Does this key child recognise their place in the family, friends, neighbourhood and the world?

Is there a particular aspect of this key child that you know less about?

How will you get this information? Through observations of the key child, talking to other staff or parents?

How do the adults support the Personal, Social and Emotional Development of their key children?

Think about all the children in your key group, and give yourself an overall score for each section on the scale below:

Dispositions and Attitudes

Do you?

- Interact with each child to support their interests?
- Encourage each child to learn from their mistakes?
- Encourage each child to think of adults as partners in learning?
- Challenge each child's negative comments and actions to adults or peers?
- Teach each child to look after resources and trust them to do this independently?
- Let each child finish activities until they are happy with them?
- Encourage each child to talk about their learning and value their ideas?
- Provide challenging but achievable activities?
- Explain to each child why it is important to pay attention when listening to others?

1	2	3	4	5

Just beginning to...   Doing it all!

Self-confidence and Self-esteem

Do you?

- Give extra support to each child in new situations?
- Plan in extra time to help each child with transitions within or beyond the setting?
- Listen to parents, offer information and support?
- Encourage each child to talk and listen to each other about their homes and community life?
- Ensure each child learning English as an additional language has opportunities to express themselves in their home language?
- Anticipate the best from each child and know their strengths?
- Support each child in talking about a range of feelings and explain to others why they feel that way?
- Give each child who needs it extra help or support to meet their individual needs?
- Help each child and parents see that their cultures and beliefs are similar?

1	2	3	4	5

Just beginning to...   Doing it all!

Making Relationships

Do you?

- Encourage each child to play with a range of friends so everyone feels included?
- Have a predictable sequence to the routine and prepare each child for changes in it?
- Have stability in the staffing and grouping of children?
- Involve each child in agreeing the codes for behaviour and to be responsible for implementing them?

1	2	3	4	5

Just beginning to...   Doing it all!

continued on next sheet

Personal, Social and Emotional Development

How do the adults support the Personal, Social and Emotional Development of their key children? *(cont.)*

Think about all the children in your key group, and give yourself an overall score for each section on the scale below:

Behaviour and Self-control

Do you?

- Share with parents and each child the reasons for the boundaries and expectations to support a joint approach?
- Collaborate with each child on the rules for looking after the environment?
- Affirm and praise positive behaviour explaining it makes people happy?
- Encourage each child to think about issues from the viewpoint of others?
- Help each child understand what is right and wrong?
- Involve each child in identifying issues and finding solutions?
- Notice injustices and let each child see they are addressed and resolved?

1	2	3	4	5

Just beginning to...   Doing it all!

Self-care

Do you?

- Plan opportunities for each child to take the initiative in their learning?
- Build on each child's ideas to plan new experiences that present challenges?
- Give each child opportunities to be responsible to set up and clear away activities?
- Give each child time to try before intervening to support and guide them?
- Have an atmosphere where achievement is valued?
- Encourage each child to solve their own problems and support this by clarifying the problem with them?

1	2	3	4	5

Just beginning to...   Doing it all!

Sense of Community

Do you?

- Encourage each child to build relationships with community members, for example, fire fighters who visit the setting?
- Have opportunities for each child to be curious, engaged, enthusiastic and tranquil?
- Ensure every child is given the support necessary to participate in discussions and be listened to?
- Encourage each child to discuss their similarities and differences in their experiences and the reasons for these?

1	2	3	4	5

Just beginning to...   Doing it all!

Who do you need to know more about?

Is there a particular aspect of the children's day and lives that you want to develop?

Resources and experiences that promote Personal, Social and Emotional Development.

Think about your environment. Do you have:

Dispositions and Attitudes

- A range of activities so the children are introduced to different materials, indoors and outdoors?
- Accessible materials for all the children so they can make choices?
- Time for the children to pursue activities and return to them?
- Time for the children to tell a group of children about things they have done or sing a song?

Self-confidence and Self-esteem

- Role play areas with a variety of resources reflecting diversity?
- A display showing all the people who make up the 'community' of the setting?
- Props to help the children show how they feel, for example a sad puppet?
- A diary of experiences that is shared with the children to help them recall when they have felt happy, lonely, sad, excited?
- Stories that reflect the diversity of the children's experiences?
- Information to help the children understand and talk about why people do things differently or similarly to each other?
- People visiting who are from a range of cultural backgrounds to talk about their lives or what they do in their job, for example, someone familiar with local area?

Making Relationships

- Time, materials and space for the children to collaborate, for example, on a construction?
- A role play area that reflects the children's lives and communities?
- Activities that promote turn-taking and sharing?

Behaviour and Self-control

- Pets/plants/toys that the children can respect and care for?
- Books with stories about characters that follow or break the rules and the effects this has on others?
- Clear, consistent, reasonable limits for behaviour that the children know and understand?
- Time to listen to children raising injustices to come to a 'best fit' solution, for example, sharing the best bicycle?

Self-care

- Ways to praise the children's efforts for managing their personal needs and looking after resources?
- Means for the children to keep track of and share their achievements with others, for example, portfolios?
- Opportunities for self-chosen activities and choices within adult-led activities?

Sense of Community

- Activities where the children share experiences and knowledge from different parts of their lives with each other?
- Resources to help all the children participate fully, for example, an interpreter for children learning English as an additional language?
- Positive images of the children's own cultures and faiths and those of others?
- Props for telling stories that support the children to tell stories about their own experiences and others?

Rate your environment from 1–5

1	2	3	4	5
Just beginning to enable				Very enabling environment

How could you improve your environment and make it even more enabling for Personal, Social and Emotional Development?

Let's look at the Communication, Language and Literacy of your unique key children.

Read the following questions and think about each key child in your group as you read each one. Remember the many ways babies communicate and respond by eye contact, grasping, head-turning, wiggling toes, smiling, banging, vocalising and facial expressions.

How much do you know about _____ (key child's name)?

- How this baby communicates?
- When does this baby listen and makes sounds?
- This baby's early words in their preferred language?
- How this baby responds to new events and experiences around them?
- How much this baby understands?
- How this baby shows their understanding?
- This baby's personal words and sounds to label people and things that are important to them?
- The ways and signs that this baby makes when they are listening?
- The songs and rhymes that this baby enjoys and likes?
- What kind of objects does this baby grasp and reach for?
- How this baby makes marks, for example, rubbing a rusk on the highchair?
- How this baby prefers to play, with their fingers and toes or objects?
- What are the sounds and movements this baby makes when exploring and playing?

Is there a particular aspect of this baby that you know less about?

How will you get this information? Through observations of the baby, talking to other staff or parents?

How do the adults support the Communication, Language and Literacy development of their key children?

Think about all the babies in your key group, and give yourself an overall score for each section on the scale below:

Do you?

- Use your voice, eye contact and touch to have 'chats' with each baby?
- Use each baby's name?
- Use key words from each baby's home language?
- Tell stories, rhymes and sing songs from a range of cultures utilising each baby's home languages?
- 'Tune in' and interpret what each baby is communicating to you or others?
- Use the greetings and words with each baby that their family uses at home?
- Show an interest in what each baby is interested in, looking at and playing with?
- Talk about what you're doing to each baby such making the lunch or changing a nappy?
- Encourage each baby to turn-take with you in rhymes like 'Row, row your boat' and games like Peek-a-boo?
- Respond to each baby's words and communication?
- Tell and read stories to each baby at different times of the day such as before a sleep?
- Talk about and value the early marks made by each baby?
- Talk about the movements each baby makes such as round and round?
- Let each baby have the freedom to move and grasp toys?

1	2	3	4	5

Just beginning to...   Doing it all!

Do you discuss with parents (using support/translation as needed):

- Their preferred language(s) used at home to communicate with their baby?
- The greetings they use with their baby at home?
- The copying games such as Peek-a-boo that the babies and their families play at home?
- Each baby's special and personal words such as 'do-do' for dummy?
- The rhymes and songs they sing to their babies at home?

1	2	3	4	5

Just beginning to...   Doing it all!

Who do you need to know more about?

Is there a particular aspect of the babies' day and lives that you want to develop?

Resources and experiences that promote Communication Language and Literacy development.

Think about your environment. Do you have:

- Photographs of the natural 'signs' the babies use to communicate, for example, when they are tired or want more?

- Tape recorders and tapes so parents can record familiar sounds and songs from home to help soothe the babies?

- Stories, books, rhymes and songs from a range of cultures and ensure these include each babies' preferred language?

- Displays showing each baby's home language?

- A communication system to exchange information with parents on the babies' personal words and signs?

- Resources that stimulate and interest babies?

- An environment that the babies can respond to through touching, smiling, smelling, feeling, listening, exploring and sharing?

- Times that you sing with the babies?

- Lists of each baby's personal words from home and in the setting?

- A range of board books, cloth books and stories that interest the babies?

- Gloop, paint and other tactile materials for the babies to make marks with?

- Toys that the babies can reach and grasp?

- Activities that encourage the babies to move their bodies, arms, legs, hands and feet such as balls and push-along toys?

- Arrange the environment so that the babies can pull themselves up and 'walk' between furniture placed at a safe distance?

Rate your environment from 1–5

1	2	3	4	5

Just beginning to enable   Very enabling environment

How could you improve your environment and make it even more enabling for Communication, Language and Literacy?

The EYFS: Am I getting it right? © Anita Soni & Sue Bristow

Let's look at the Communication, Language and Literacy of your unique children.

Read the following questions and think about each key child in your group as you read each one.

How much do you know about _____ (key child's name)?

Language for Communication

- The words this key child can use and understand?
- When this key child tends to use their home language, for example, when they are excited?
- The type of questions this key child tends to ask?
- When and how this key child prefers to interact and communicate with adults?

Language for Thinking

- How and when this key child is likely to respond to adults or other children?
- When this key child will communicate using actions or words?
- The ways this key child will communicate with others, for example, by asking questions, using words or actions or signs?

Linking Sounds and Letters

- This key child's favourite words and phrases?
- The languages this key child uses or understands?

Reading

- How this key child responds to books and stories?
- This key child's favourite songs, rhymes, stories, poems and jingles?

Writing

- When this key child is likely to make marks, for example, with a crayon or a brush, in sand, in water or clay?
- What this key child says about their marks? Do they say what it is or not?

Handwriting

- How well this key child is developing fine motor control, for example, using zips, doing buttons or pouring a drink?

Is there a particular aspect of the child that you know less about?

How will you get this information? Through observations of the key child, talking to other staff or parents?

Communication, Language and Literacy

How do the adults support the Communication, Language and Literacy of their key children?

Think about all the children in your key group, and give yourself an overall score for each section on the scale below:

Do you?

- Appreciate each child's efforts when they understand new words/phrases?
- Gently demonstrate how to pronounce the words and order the words in sentences after each child has spoken rather than correcting them?
- Praise when each child speaks in their home language and give English versions too?
- Comment on each child's play to give a demonstration of structures in speech, for example, I catch the ball, you catch the ball, Naima catches the ball?
- Talk about things that interest each child?
- Listen and respond to each child's ideas and questions that may be given in home languages or non-verbally as well as verbally?
- Recognise that each child can often understand more than they can say?
- Give a running commentary on each child's play?
- Give opportunities for each child to talk with other children and adults?
- Encourage each child to learn and pronounce their own name and everyone's name correctly?
- Encourage each child to play and explore sounds, for example, making the 'chug chug' noise of a tractor in a story or song?
- Encourage each child to join in with rhyme, rhythm and repetition in songs, poems, rhymes and stories?
- Use stories and rhymes from a range of cultures?
- Consider the needs of each child who have English as an additional language?
- Tell and read stories to each child with different voices, with and without props?
- Discuss what each child has drawn and written?
- Talk about what signs and symbols (in English and other languages) say?
- Help each child develop their fine motor skills by doing activities such as scribbling, rolling, printing and tearing?
- Encourage each child to use a range of media and implements, for example, clay, fingerpaint, brushes, shells and so on?

1	2	3	4	5

Just beginning to...   Doing it all!

Do you discuss with parents (using support/translation as needed):

- The rhymes they sing at home (in home languages too)?
- The stories they read at home (in home languages too)?
- The correct way of pronouncing the names of their children and their own?
- The value of parents continuing to use their first language at home?

1	2	3	4	5

Just beginning to...   Doing it all!

Who do you need to know more about?

Is there a particular aspect of the children's day and lives that you want to develop?

Resources and experiences that promote Communication, Language and Literacy.

Think about your environment. Do you have:

- Books and stories with repetitive phrases?
- Time to follow the children's lead and have fun together while talking about actions such as up and down?
- Photographs showing familiar events, objects and activities from home and the setting and talk about them with the children?
- Activities and resources that encourage symbolic play, for example, babies to put to bed?
- Activities, experiences and resources that excite the children's curiosity?
- Activities and experiences, for example, cooking, planting to anticipate what comes next?
- Resources that the children can listen to and distinguish between such as musical instruments?
- Puppets and other props to encourage listening and responding to stories and songs?
- Stories, pictures and puppets where you can talk about how the character feels?
- CDs and tapes of rhymes, stories, spoken words and songs?
- Dual language books, CDs and tapes that include the home languages of the children to show an awareness of other languages and scripts?
- A range of mark-making materials?
- Materials with writing from other languages, such as calendars?
- Resources for finger painting and play to allow the children to make marks?
- A range of tools for the children to use to develop fine motor skills, for example, rakes and sticks in the sand?

Rate your environment from 1–5

1	2	3	4	5

Just beginning to enable   Very enabling environment

How could you improve your environment and make it even more enabling for Communication, Language and Literacy?

Communication, Language and Literacy

Communication, Language and Literacy

Let's look at the Communication, Language and Literacy of your unique children.

Read the following questions and think about each key child in your group as you read each one.

How much do you know about _____ (key child's name)?

Language for Communication
- How this key child responds to stories and information books you read to them?
- Does this key child act out stories and rhymes?
- Does this key child recall and recount their own experiences and share them with others?
- Who (children or adults) this key child likes to have conversations with?
- How complicated an instruction this key child can follow?
- What type of question this key child tends to ask?
- The range and variety of words this key child uses?
- Does this key child develop stories or explain what they are saying to others?
- When will this key child choose to talk, for example, to get attention or solve a problem?
- The rhymes and songs this key child knows and likes?
- Does this key child make up songs of their own?
- Is this key child able to consider the needs of the listener, for example, looking at them, changing style for younger children?

Language for Thinking
- The type of talk this key child uses to give a running commentary as they play?
- Does this key child use talk to connect ideas and explain things, for example, it's too windy today so we won't play out as we might blow away?
- Does this key child talk about past experiences?
- How does this key child talk about their feelings?
- The ways this key child uses language in imaginative play?
- When this key child is likely to use their home language and likely to use English?

Linking Sounds and Letters
- Can this key child make up rhymes to words?
- Can this key child hear the rhythm in words such as tapping out the syllables?
- Can this key child make up different versions of favourite rhymes?
- What significant letters does this key child recognises, for example, letters in own name?
- How this key child uses their knowledge of letters to read and write?

Reading
- This key child's favourite stories and poems that they can retell?
- How much this key child knows about how books and stories work, for example, the beginning and the ending?
- How much this key child shows about understanding print can be read?
- What this key child can recognise/read, for example, their name, other letters, words?
- This key child's favourite books?
- How this key child uses non-fiction books?
- The phonic skills and strategies this key child uses to read?
- How confident this key child is to have a go at reading?

Writing
- The marks this key child makes and the meanings given to them?
- How this key child uses writing to record things and communicates?
- The different types of writing this key child will do such as labels, letters, and lists?
- The knowledge of writing and phonics that this key child uses to write sentences?

Handwriting
- The ways this key child can control equipment and materials?
- The marks this key child likes to make?
- How well this key child can manipulate a range of tools in their play and writing?
- The letters and words this key child can write?

Is there a particular aspect of this key child that you know less about?

How will you get this information? Observations of the key child, talk to other staff or parents?

How do the adults support the Communication, Language and Literacy of their key children?

Think about all the children in your key group, and give yourself an overall score for each section on the scale below:

Language for Communication

Do you?

- Talk with each child to make links between their gestures and words, for example, 'You look a bit sad, has someone upset you?'
- Use a variety of communication strategies including signing as appropriate?
- Show that you listen to each child in your responses?
- Tell and read stories with repeated refrains?
- Sing songs with actions and replies such as 'Tommy Thumb'?
- Tell a range of rhymes from different cultures?
- Give clear instructions?
- Use gesture and photographs to help understanding when needed?
- Have activities that encourage each child to ask and answer questions?
- Introduce new words regularly through play and activities?
- Show interest in the words each child uses to communicate and describe their experiences?
- Expand on what each child says to develop more complex sentences?
- Role model how to talk appropriately with correct grammar to others such as listening, waiting for the other person to finish, saying please and thank you?
- Demonstrate language to negotiate such as 'May I...' or 'I think...'?
- Model the different language used for different audiences, for example, younger children?
- Encourage and help each child to predict endings to stories?
- Encourage each child to play with stories, sounds and words?
- Value each child's ideas and contributions to discussions?

1	2	3	4	5

Just beginning to...   Doing it all!

Language for Thinking

Do you?

- Get involved in each child's play to promote their thinking and discussion?
- Talk to each child about what they have been doing and help them explain?
- Ask each child to predict how they will do a task?
- Ask each child to predict endings to stories or explain stories?
- Help each child to see patterns in stories and explain events?
- Take an interest in each child's ideas and thoughts?

1	2	3	4	5

Just beginning to...   Doing it all!

Linking Sounds and Letters

Do you?

- Ask each child to think of other rhyming words for rhymes and songs?
- Talk to each child about letters in important words such as their names?
- Role-model writing to show how to spell and write?
- Encourage each child to use the letters they know in words?

1	2	3	4	5

Just beginning to...   Doing it all!

continued on next sheet

Communication, Language and Literacy

Communication, Language and Literacy

How do the adults support the Communication, Language and Literacy of their key children? *(cont.)*

Think about all the children in your key group, and give yourself an overall score for each section on the scale below:

Reading

Do you?

- Encourage each child to use stories and the main events within them in their play?
- Discuss the characters in books and stories with each child?
- Encourage each child to compare the stories to their own experiences and feelings?
- Use print that is important to each child such as their names and favourite foods to look at letters and words?
- Point out words in books, on labels and signs?
- Read familiar stories to each child, letting them 'read' the next word or phrase?
- Make up words to describe characters in stories?
- Discuss and model finding information from books?
- Talk to parents about the value of reading including using environmental print and their children's favourite books?
- Show children how to use phonics to read words?
- Encourage each child to read words they see a lot, such as their name, friends' names?
- Play word games to develop recognition of words seen a lot?

1	2	3	4	5

Just beginning to...   Doing it all!

Writing

Do you?

- Write poems and stories with each child?
- Support each child to recognise and write their names?
- Encourage each child to use their knowledge of letters to write words?
- Scribe (say each word as you write it down including punctuation) what each child says, for example, when labelling pictures?
- Play games to help each child hear the sounds at the beginning of words, and then the order in which they occur?
- Play games to link sounds and letters, and write letters and words?
- Encourage each child to read out what they have written?

1	2	3	4	5

Just beginning to...   Doing it all!

Handwriting

Do you?

- Have activities to promote manipulative skills like cooking, playing instruments?
- Show each child how to form letters correctly such as when they label pictures?
- Encourage each child to practise writing letters as they play, write, paint and draw?
- Have opportunities for each child to write in imaginative play?

1	2	3	4	5

Just beginning to...   Doing it all!

Who do you need to know more about?

Is there a particular aspect of the children's day and lives that you want to develop?

Resources and experiences that promote Communication, Language and Literacy.

Think about your environment. Do you have:

Language for Communication
- A listening area where the children can enjoy rhymes and songs?
- Rhyme bags containing rhyme and songs to take home?
- Copies of parents' songs that you can play to the children?
- Story props, for example, puppets and objects to help the children retell stories?
- Time for the children to talk, discuss and share?
- Time for the children to think before answering?
- Joint activities for a group of children to help them talk, plan and decide?
- Exciting and stimulating play opportunities to talk about?
- Writing materials and word banks inside and outside?
- Listening and writing materials in the role play areas inside and outside?
- Activities where the children really need to speak and listen such as showing pictures to others?

Language for Thinking
- Photographs of shared experiences for the children to look at and talk about?
- Props and materials to help children re-enact events?
- Objects, photographs and artefacts to remind the children of activities they have experienced?
- Imaginative play to encourage the children to act out scenarios in character?

Linking Sounds and Letters
- Examples of printed and written writing in the role play areas?
- Fun word games and activities that show how words rhyme?
- Programme of systematic phonic work for the children when the practitioner thinks they are ready (generally when the children are five)?

Reading
- An attractive book area for the children and adults to read in together?
- Poetry, song, fiction and non-fiction available?
- Books and stories with photographs of the children in?
- Print in the environment to help the children learn about words?
- Print on information and instruction leaflets for the children to look at?
- Story props to support the children's understanding of stories?
- Bilingual story times?
- ICT to support reading, for example, Living Books?
- Story boards so children can talk about the sequence of stories?
- Story sacks for the setting and home?
- Some simple text that children can 'read' themselves containing familiar words?
- Picture books, books with flaps, books with CDs and tapes?

Writing
- Activities where the children can experiment with writing such as a message board?
- Opportunities and materials for writing in a range of activities including role play?
- Word banks and resources for segmenting and blending to support the children in using their phonic knowledge?

Handwriting
- Large shoulder movement opportunities such as ribbon swirling, batting balls?
- Materials to enable the children to make shapes on the floor and in the air, such as sand and water?
- A variety of writing materials and paper, both indoor and out?
- Opportunities to write meaningfully such as having notebooks and calendars?

Rate your environment from 1–5

1	2	3	4	5
Just beginning to enable				Very enabling environment

How could you improve your environment and make it even more enabling for Communication, Language and Literacy?

Communication, Language and Literacy

Let's look at the Problem Solving, Reasoning and Numeracy of your unique key children.

Read the following questions and think about each key child in your group as you read each one.

How much do you know about _____ (key child's name)?

- How this baby responds to people and objects?
- Does this baby notice changes in groupings of objects, images and sounds?
- What this baby's favourite number rhyme and action song is?
- How this baby responds to favourite things?
- How this baby responds when playing games that involve objects being shown, then hidden away?
- How this baby responds when things disappear from sight?
- How this baby persists in trying to achieve something they have managed before?
- How this baby explores the space around them?
- How this baby is beginning to be aware of distance?
- How this baby investigates objects and space?
- What this baby does when picking up objects of different sizes, for example, holding out arms wide to pick up a big teddy?

Is there a particular aspect of this key child that you know less about?

How will you get this information? Through observations of the baby, talking to other staff or parents?

How do the adults support the Problem Solving, Reasoning and Numeracy of their key children?

Think about all the babies in your key group, and give yourself an overall score for each section on the scale below:

Do you?

- Identify the people, toys and experiences that each baby enjoys?
- Talk about the things that each baby notices when they are in different places?
- Sing number rhymes as you dress or change each baby?
- Move with each baby to the rhythm patterns in familiar songs and rhymes?
- Encourage each baby to join in tapping and clapping along to simple rhythms?
- Talk to each baby about what you are doing and what is happening?
- Play games such as peek-a-boo or comment when a puppet pops out of a sock?
- Talk to each baby about puzzles they may encounter such as when a toy falls out of their reach?
- Have conversations about things that interest them which includes describing particular features?
- Play games with each baby that involve curling and stretching, popping up and bobbing down?
- Encourage each baby to explore the characteristics of objects?
- Talk about what objects are like and how objects can change their shape by being squeezed or stretched?

1	2	3	4	5

Just beginning to...   Doing it all!

Do you discuss with parents (using support/translation as needed):

- What number songs and rhymes they sing at home?

1	2	3	4	5

Just beginning to...   Doing it all!

Who do you need to know more about?

Is there a particular aspect of the babies' day and lives that you want to develop?

Problem Solving, Reasoning and Numeracy

Resources and experiences that promote Problem Solving, Reasoning and Numeracy.

Think about your environment. Do you have:

- Displays of each baby's favourite things in a lively and attractive environment?
- A small group of same objects in treasure baskets as well as single items?
- A collection of number rhymes which are repetitive and are related to children's actions?
- A collection of songs and rhymes for use during personal routines?
- A collection of number and counting rhymes from a range of cultures and in different languages?
- Lift-the-flap books?
- A variety of interesting displays for the babies to see when looking around them, looking at the ceiling or peering around the corner?
- Displays of things to look at that encourage their interest in movement such as spirals?
- A range of objects of various weights and textures in treasure baskets that excites and encourages the babies' interests?
- Books showing objects such as a big car and a little car?
- Story props to support all children and particularly those learning English as an additional language?

Rate your environment from 1–5

1	2	3	4	5
Just beginning to enable				Very enabling environment

How could you improve your environment and make it even more enabling for Problem Solving, Reasoning and Numeracy?

Let's look at Problem Solving, Reasoning and Numeracy of your unique key children.

Read the following questions and think about each key child in your group as you read each one.

How much do you know about _____ (key child's name)?

Numbers as Labels and for Counting

- What this key child's awareness of number is such as the number words used in play and when and why they use them?
- Whether this key child notices and/or chooses objects based on quantity, for example, more, most?
- Does this key child show an understanding of number as labels such as 1,2,3?
- Which situations prompt this key child to talk about numbers?
- Which numbers this key child recites spontaneously in their games?
- Whether this key child can match one thing with another, for example, cup and saucer?

Calculating

- When this key child gathers a collection of objects together, for example, lining up cars, collecting leaves?
- Whether this key child is interested in helping when an adult is sorting fruit at snack time or tidying up the toys?
- Whether this key child can make deductions about whether there is some juice left or whether it is all gone?
- Does this key child attempt to estimate and then check number by counting?
- How this key child reacts during simple counting songs?
- What this key child knows about dividing things equally into two groups?

Shape, Space and Measures

- What strategies this key child uses as they select and fit shapes in a puzzle or balance blocks on one another?
- What shapes of everyday objects is this key child interested in?
- What this key child notices about shapes or patterns?
- What words this key child is beginning to use that describe time, amount and size?

Is there a particular aspect of this key child that you know less about?

How will you get this information? Through observations of the key child, talking to other staff or parents?

Problem Solving, Reasoning and Numeracy

How do the adults support the Problem Solving, Reasoning and Numeracy of their key children?

Think about the children in your key group and give yourself a score from 1–5 on the scale below:

Do you?

- Use number names in meaningful contexts?
- Talk about 'lots' and 'few' as the children play?
- Give each child opportunities to practise one-to-one correspondence in real life situations?
- Talk about the maths in everyday situations?
- Show each child how we use counting to find out 'how many'?
- Talk about how the symbols and marks you make stand for numbers and quantities?
- Ask questions such as 'would you like one sandwich or two?'
- Talk about portions of food so that each child learns about quantities?
- Foster each child's ability to classify and compare amounts?
- Use 'tidy up time' to promote logic and reasoning about where things fit in and are kept?
- Help each child organise their ideas by talking to them about what they are doing?
- Play games which relate to number order, addition and subtraction such as hopscotch and skittles?
- Sing counting songs and rhymes which help to develop each child's understanding of number?
- Talk to each child, as they play with water or sand, to encourage them to think about when something is full, empty or holds more?
- Help each child to create different arrangements in the layout of road and rail tracks?
- Highlight patterns in daily activities and routines?
- Help each child to touch, see and feel shape through art, music and dance?
- Encourage each child to create their own patterns in art, music and dance?
- Talk about and help each child to recognise patterns?
- Draw each child's attention to the pattern of square/oblong/square which emerges as you fold or unfold a tablecloth or napkin?
- Use consistent vocabulary for weight and mass, for example, heavy and light?
- Sort coins on play trays into interesting arrangements and shapes; sort them into bags, purses and containers?
- Measure for a purpose, such as finding out whether a teddy will fit in a bed?

1	2	3	4	5

Just beginning to...   Doing it all!

Do you discuss with parents (using support/translation as needed):

- The ways children learn about numbers in your setting?
- The importance of talking in their home language about quantities and numbers?

1	2	3	4	5

Just beginning to...   Doing it all!

Who do you need to know more about?

Is there a particular aspect of the children's day and lives that you want to develop?

The EYFS: Am I getting it right? © Anita Soni & Sue Bristow

Resources and experiences that promote Problem Solving, Reasoning and Numeracy.

Think about your environment. Do you have:

- Varied opportunities to explore 'lots' and 'few' in play?

- A role-play area equipped with things that can be sorted in different ways?

- Collections of objects that can be sorted and matched in various ways?

- Resources that support the children in making one-to-one correspondences, for example giving each dolly a cup of tea?

- Number labels to use outdoors for car number plates, house and bus numbers?

- Resources with numbers on in the home play area, for example, a telephone directory?

- Opportunities for the children to sort foodstuffs during domestic tasks?

- Pictures or shapes of objects to indicate where things are kept?

- Props for the children to act out counting songs and rhymes?

- Games and equipment that offer opportunities for counting, such as skittles?

- Opportunities for the children to explore 'maths' in areas such as the sand, water or other play areas?

- Different sizes and shapes of containers in water play, so that the children can experiment with quantities and measures?

- A range of puzzles with large pieces and knobs or handles to support success in fitting shapes into spaces?

- Pictures that illustrate the use of shapes and patterns from a variety of cultures, for example, Arabic designs?

- Opportunities for children to measure time (sand timer), weight (balance) and measure (non-standard units)?

- Opportunities to vary the use of volume and capacity equipment in the sand, water and other play areas to maintain interest?

Rate your environment from 1–5

1	2	3	4	5

Just beginning to enable   Very enabling environment

How could you improve your environment and make it even more enabling for Problem Solving, Reasoning and Numeracy?

Problem Solving, Reasoning and Numeracy

Let's look at the Problem Solving, Reasoning and Numeracy of your unique key children.

Read the following questions and think about each key child in your group as you read each one.

How much do you know about _____ **(key child's name)?**

Numbers as Labels and for Counting
- Does this key child know that different numbers have different names?
- Does this key child use the names for numbers accurately?
- What is the range of numbers that this key child refers to, and why do they use these numbers?
- Can this key child estimate and check their guess?
- Can this key child accurately use ordinals, for example, first, second, third and so on?
- What strategies this key child uses to match number and quantity, for example, using fingers or tally by making marks?
- What personal numbers this key child refers to, for example, their age, house number?
- Whether there are instances of this key child counting an irregular arrangement of up to ten objects?
- What this key child's methods are for counting out up to six objects from a larger group, for example, sharing out pieces of a jigsaw and counting to check everyone has the same number?
- How this key child has begun to represent numbers using fingers, marks on paper or pictures?
- Whether this key child recognises any numerals and which ones they know?
- How this key child uses their developing understanding of maths to solve mathematical problems?

Calculating
- What strategies this key child uses to work out whether a group of objects is the same or different?
- How this key child works out a solution to a simple problem, for example, by using fingers or counting aloud?
- What methods this key child uses to answer a problem they have posed, for example, 'Get one more, and then we will both have two'?
- How this key child finds the sum of two numbers?
- Which ways this key child counts repeated groups of the same size, for example, counting the numbers of socks in five pairs?
- Whether this key child can share objects into equal groups and count how many are in each group?
- Whether this key child can work out what remains if something is taken away?

Shape, Space and Measures
- Whether this key child shows an interest in shape and space by playing with shapes or making arrangements with objects?
- Whether this key child recognises shapes in the environment, for example, that a roof has a triangle at one end?
- Whether this key child is beginning to understand 'bigger than' and 'enough'?
- How this key child applies their understanding of shape and space, for example, knowing they need one flat shape and one that is pointy?
- Whether this key child uses mathematical names for shapes, such as 'circle' and 'triangle'?
- Whether this key child shows curiosity about shapes by talking about similarities and differences?
- Whether this key child can match some shapes by recognising similarities and orientation, for example, Stevie looked at a rhomboid, saying, 'It looks like a boat'.
- Whether this key child can select a named shape for a particular purpose?
- Whether this key child can use positional and/or directional clues, for example, 'We had to come round the park and past the shops'?
- Whether this key child can order two items by length or height, for example, compare the length of zips on coats: 'Too long for your coat'?
- Whether this key child can identify a mathematical problem involving shape, space or measures and find ways to solve it?
- Whether this key child can use positional language, such as 'I am on the bike'?
- What words this key child uses to describe comparisons and measures such as 'greater', 'smaller', 'heavier' or 'lighter'?

Is there a particular aspect of this key child that you know less about?
How will you get this information? Through observations of the key child, talking to other staff or parents?

How do the adults support the Problem Solving, Reasoning and Numeracy of their key children?

Think about all the children in your key group, and give yourself an overall score for each section on the scale below:

Numbers as Labels and for Counting
Do you?
- Use number language, for example, 'one', 'two', 'lots', 'hundreds' and count in a variety of situations?
- Model and encourage use of mathematical language by, for example, asking questions such as, 'How many saucepans will fit on the shelf?'
- Allow each child to understand that one thing can be shared, for example, a pizza?
- Encourage estimation, for example, estimate how many sandwiches to make for the picnic?
- Ensure that each child is involved in making displays, such as making their own pictograms of lunch choices?
- Add numerals to all areas of the curriculum, for example to a display of a favourite story such as *The Three Billy Goats Gruff*?
- Make books about numbers that have meaning for each child such as favourite numbers, birth dates or telephone numbers?
- Use rhymes, songs and stories involving counting on and counting back in ones, twos, fives and tens?
- Emphasise the empty set and introduce the concept of nothing or zero?

1	2	3	4	5

Just beginning to...   Doing it all!

Calculating
Do you?
- Demonstrate language such as 'same as' 'less' or 'fewer'?
- As you read number stories or rhymes, ask, for example, 'How many will there be in the pool when one more frog jumps in?'
- Use pictures and objects to illustrate counting songs, rhymes and number stories?
- Show interest in how each child solves problems and value their different solutions?
- Make sure each child is secure about the order of numbers before asking what comes after or before each number?
- Discuss with each child how problems relate to others they have met, and their different solutions?
- Encourage each child to make up their own story problems for other children to solve?
- Encourage each child to extend problems, for example, 'Suppose there were three people to share the bricks between instead of two'?
- Use mathematical vocabulary and demonstrate methods of recording, using standards notation where appropriate?
- Give each child learning English as an additional language opportunities to work in their home language to ensure accurate understanding of concepts?

1	2	3	4	5

Just beginning to...   Doing it all!

Shape, Space and Measures
Do you?
- Demonstrate the language for shape, position and measures in discussions, for example, 'ball shape', 'box shape', 'inside', 'heavy', 'full' and 'longer' and find out and use equivalent terms for these measures in home languages?
- Encourage each child to talk about the shapes they see and use and how they are arranged?
- Value each child's constructions by helping them display them or take a photograph of them?
- Organise the environment to foster shape-matching, for example, pictures of different bricks on containers to show where they are kept?
- Ask 'silly' questions, for example, show a tiny box and ask if there is a bicycle in it?
- Make books about shape, time and measures, for example, shapes found in the environment?
- Introduce each child to the use of mathematical names for 'solid' 3-D shapes and 'flat' 2-D shapes, and the mathematical terms to describe shapes?
- Ensure each child uses everyday words to describe position, for example, when following pathways or playing with outdoor apparatus?

1	2	3	4	5

Just beginning to...   Doing it all!

Who do you need to know more about?
Is there a particular aspect of the children's day and lives that you want to develop?

Problem Solving, Reasoning and Numeracy

Resources and experiences that promote Problem Solving, Reasoning and Numeracy.

Think about your environment. Do you have:

Numbers as Labels and for Counting
- Opportunities for the children to have a reason to count?
- Opportunities for the children to note the missing set, for example, 'There are none left' when sharing things out?
- Number labels for the children to use, for example, by putting a number label on each bike and a corresponding number on each parking space?
- Counting money and change in role play games?
- Collections of interesting things for the children to sort, order, count and label in their play?
- Numerals displayed in purposeful contexts?
- Tactile numeral cards made from sandpaper, velvet or string?
- Opportunities for the children to experiment with a number of objects, the written numeral and the written number name?
- A 100 square for the children's use to explore number patterns?
- A display of interesting books about number?
- Opportunities for the children to play games such as hide and seek that involve counting?
- Opportunities for the children to count on and count back using rhymes, songs and stories?

Calculating
- Opportunities for the children to separate objects into unequal groups as well as equal groups?
- Story props that the children can use in their play, for example, a variety of fruits and baskets like Handa in the story *Handa's Surprise* by Eileen Browne (Walker Books Ltd)?
- Opportunities for the children to record what they have done, for example, by drawing or tallying?
- Number staircases to show a starting point and how you arrive at another point when something is added and taken away?
- A wide range of number resources to encourage the children to be creative in thinking up problems and solutions in all areas of Learning and Development?
- Opportunities for the children to make links between cardinal numbers (quantity) and ordinal numbers (position)?
- Have number lines available for reference and encourage the children to use them in their own play?
- Opportunities for the children to understand that five fingers on each hand make a total of ten fingers altogether, or that two rows of three eggs in the box makes six altogether?

Shape, Space and Measures
- Large and small blocks and boxes available for construction both indoors and outdoors?
- Opportunities to play games involving the children positioning themselves inside, behind, on top and so on?
- Rich and varied opportunities for comparing length, weight and time?
- Stories such as Rosie's Walk by Pat Hutchins (Red Fox) to talk about distance and stimulate discussion about non-standard units and the need for standard units?
- Pictures that have symmetry or pattern and talk to the children about them?
- A range of boxes and materials for models and constructions such as 'dens', indoors and outdoors?
- Examples of the same shape in different sizes?
- Areas where the children can explore the properties of objects and where they can weigh and measure, such as a cookery station or a building area?
- Opportunities for the children to describe and compare shapes, measures and distance?
- Materials and resources for the children to observe and describe patterns in the indoor and outdoor environment and in daily routines, orally, in pictures or using objects?
- A range of natural materials for the children to arrange, compare and order?

Rate your environment from 1–5

1	2	3	4	5

Just beginning to enable

Very enabling environment

How could you improve your environment and make it even more enabling for Problem Solving, Reasoning and Numeracy?

Let's look at the development of Knowledge and Understanding of the World of your unique key children.

Read the following questions and think about each key child in your group as you read each one. Remember the many ways babies communicate and respond by eye contact, grasping, head-turning, wiggling toes, smiling, banging, vocalising and facial expressions.

How much do you know about _____ (key child's name)?

- How this baby uses their senses to investigate such things as your face, your hair, a rattle?
- What ways this baby investigates and manipulates objects?
- What objects interest and engage this baby's attention?
- How this baby handles and arranges objects such as blocks or bricks?
- Which toys and resources interest this baby?
- How this baby explores technology in toys and personal items, for example, pressing a button or lifting the spout on a drinking cup?
- How this baby reacts to sounds, sights and actions that interest them?
- Whether this baby is able to anticipate the events of the day, for example, looking out of the window when it is time to be collected?
- How this baby moves around exploring the environment?
- How this baby explores the objects and features of the environment?
- How this baby responds to your attention?
- Who this baby likes to be with (adults and children)?
- The different ways this baby responds to and communicates with adults and other children?

Is there a particular aspect of this baby that you know less about?

How will you get this information? Through observations of the baby, talking to other staff or parents?

Knowledge and Understanding of the World

How do the adults support the development of Knowledge and Understanding of the World of their key children?

Think about all the babies in your key group, and give yourself an overall score for each section on the scale below:

Do you?

- Give opportunities for each baby to explore objects and materials?

- Give choices about what each baby can play with?

- Talk to each baby about particular objects and materials, drawing their attention to features such as their feel or sound?

- Talk with each baby about the way things balance or what happens when a structure falls down?

- Talk with each baby about the features of items that interest them, for example, a toy rabbit's floppy ears?

- Talk with each baby about what you are doing as you prepare a feed or a bath?

- Spend time with each baby looking at and talking about pictures of babies eating, sleeping, bathing and playing?

- Encourage each baby's movements through interactions, for example, touching their fingers and toes and showing delight at their kicking and waving?

- Draw each baby's attention to things in different areas that stimulate interest, for example, a patterned surface?

- Provide support for each baby when they are not with their key person, to give them manageable experiences with others, for example, ensure that others know each baby's special characteristics and preferences?

- Nurture each baby's sense of themselves, while also helping them to feel that they belong to the group?

1	2	3	4	5

Just beginning to...   Doing it all!

Do you discuss with parents (using support/translation as needed):

- What you have seen their baby do and compare notes?

- Significant events in their baby's day and how these are talked about, for example, 'boboes' for sleep or bedtime, 'din-din' for dinner time?

1	2	3	4	5

Just beginning to...   Doing it all!

Who do you need to know more about?

Is there a particular aspect of the babies' day and lives that you want to develop?

Resources and experiences that promote development of Knowledge and Understanding of the World.

Think about your environment. Do you have:

- A range of everyday objects for the babies to explore and investigate?

- Varied arrangements of equipment and materials that can be used with the babies in a variety of ways to maintain interest and provide challenges?

- Objects that give the babies opportunities to explore textures, shapes and sizes?

- A range of resources that the babies can use in their play that encourages their interest in balancing and building things?

- A range of playthings that excite babies' attention, including battery-operated mobiles and wind-up radios?

- Robust resources with knobs, flaps, keys or shutters?

- Pictures or photographs of things associated with regular routines?

- Spaces that give the babies different views of their surroundings, for example, soft play area with different levels to explore?

- Opportunities to talk about photographs of the babies' special people from home and their favourite places (displayed where the babies can see them)?

- Opportunities to share some stories and songs that parents and the babies use at home?

Rate your environment from 1–5

1	2	3	4	5

Just beginning to enable   Very enabling environment

How could you improve your environment and make it even more enabling for the development of Knowledge and understanding of the World?

Knowledge and Understanding of the World

Let's look at the development of Knowledge and Understanding of the World of your unique key children.

Read the following questions and think about each key child in your group as you read each one.

How much do you know about _____ (key child's name)?

Exploration and Investigation

- The things that this key child investigates repeatedly, for example, becoming absorbed in opening and shutting?

- This key child's actions and talk, in response to what they find and the questions they ask?

Designing and Making

- The things this key child enjoys building, opening and closing or pushing and pulling?

- How this key child investigates, for example, by taking all the cushions from several areas, piling them up and jumping on top of them?

ICT

- What ways this key child investigates how to push, pull, lift or press parts of toys and domestic equipment?

- How this key child uses the control technology of toys, for example, a touch screen or remote control car?

Time

- The actions that this key child does to show they understand the sequence of routines, for example, going to the cloakroom area when you say it is time to go outdoors?

- How well this key child talks about special events they experience in the home and in the setting?

- The ways this key child shows their growing understanding of the past, for example, their familiarity with places or people previously seen?

Place

- How this key child responds to sights, sounds and smells in the environment and what they like about playing outdoors?

- What things this key child says about the environment?

Communities

- This key child's family, culture, religion, home and life beyond the setting?

Is there a particular aspect of this key child that you know less about?
How will you get this information? Through observations of the key child, talking to other staff or parents?

Knowledge and Understanding of the World

How do the adults support the development of Knowledge and Understanding of the World of their key children?

Think about all the children in your key group, and give yourself an overall score for each section on the scale below:

Do you?

- Encourage each child as they explore particular patterns of thought or movement, sometimes referred to as schemas?

- Recognise that when each child does such things as jumping in a puddle, they are engaging in investigation?

- Offer a commentary on what each child is doing, describing actions, for example, 'You nearly managed it then, by pulling that handle'.

- Recognise that each child's investigations may appear futile, but that a child may be on the brink of an amazing discovery as they meticulously place more and more things on top of one another?

- Talk about ICT apparatus, what it does, what they can do with it and how to use it safely?

- Let each child use the photocopier to copy their own pictures?

- Let each child know that you understand their routines and talk them through the things you do as you get things ready?

- Make a diary of photographs to record a special occasion?

- Use the language of time such as 'yesterday', 'tomorrow' or 'next week'?

- Encourage each child to explore puddles, trees and surfaces such as grass, concrete or pebbles?

- Tell stories about places and journeys, for example, *Whatever Next!* by Jill Murphy (Macmillan Children's Books)

- Talk to each child about the special people in their lives?

- Talk to each child about valuing all skin colour differences?

- Encourage each child to take on different roles during role-play?

- Support each child's friendships by talking to them about their characteristics, such as being kind, or fun to be with?

1	2	3	4	5
Just beginning to...				Doing it all!

Do you discuss with parents (using support/translation as needed):

- Their child's interests at home and discuss how they can be encouraged?

1	2	3	4	5
Just beginning to...				Doing it all!

Who do you need to know more about?

Is there a particular aspect of the children's day and lives that you want to develop?

Knowledge and Understanding of the World

Resources and experiences that promote development of Knowledge and Understanding of the World.

Think about your environment. Do you have:

- Materials that support particular schemas, for example, things to throw for a child who is exploring trajectory?

- Ways of including information from parents who do not speak English?

- Opportunities for investigations of the natural world within an outdoor area, for example, chimes, streamers, windmills and bubbles to investigate the effects of wind?

- A range of items to inspire the children's curiosity, ensuring their investigations are conducted safely?

- Culturally diverse artefacts and opportunities to encourage the parents to bring in culturally specific and familiar items from home to share?

- Opportunities to build on the children's particular interests by adding resources to sustain and extend their efforts?

- Technology resources that the children recognise incorporated into their play, for example, a digital camera?

- Safe equipment to play with, for example, torches, transistor radios or karaoke machines?

- Stories that focus on the sequence of routines such as getting dressed, asking 'How do I put it on?'

- Opportunities for the children to work through routines in role-play such as putting a 'baby' to bed?

- Opportunities within the outdoor area for the children to investigate features such as a mound, a path or a wall?

- Stories and information books about places such as a zoo, the beach, the playground and so on?

- Opportunities for talk with other children, visitors and adults?

- A soft toy for the children to take home overnight, in turn and talk with the children about what the toy has done during these excursions?

Rate your environment from 1–5

1	2	3	4	5

Just beginning to enable   Very enabling environment

How could you improve your environment and make it even more enabling for development of Knowledge and Understanding of the World?

Let's look at the Knowledge and Understanding of the World (KUW) of your unique key children.

Read the following questions and think about each key child in your group as you read each one.

How much do you know about _____ (key child's name)?

Exploration and Investigation
- How this key child examines objects and living things to find out more about them, for example, observing plants and animals or noticing the different materials that things are made of?
- How this key child expresses choices and preferences where verbal communication is through a language other than English?
- What changes and patterns this key child notices?
- The instances of this key child identifying features of living things or objects?
- What ways does this key child find out about things in the environment, for example, by handling something and looking at it closely?
- Instances of this key child investigating everyday events, such as why a bicycle stops when the brakes are pressed?

Designing and Making
- How this key child uses tools, such as using a stick to make holes in dough?
- How this key child links experiences and uses their knowledge to design and make things?
- How this key child's skills have developed when using tools, including tools they choose for particular tasks?
- What ways this key child makes things, for example, using card, scissors, glue, string and a hole punch to make a bag to carry some things home?
- How this key child constructs for their own purposes?
- What this key child's own assessment of fitness for purpose of their designs is and the modifications they decide to make to them?

ICT
- What skills this key child has developed as they have become familiar with simple equipment, for example, twisting and turning a knob?

Time
- What this key child has remembered about and talked about a significant event, such as finding a dead jellyfish at the beach?
- Whether this key child is able to make comparisons about what they can do now with what they could do when they were younger?
- Whether this key child is able to refer to past events?
- Whether this key child is able to compare experiences in their own life with those of others, such as comparing their own play and playthings with their grandparents' experiences of play?

Place
- Whether this key child shows an interest in things they see while out walking?
- What questions this key child asks about features of the built environment, such as. road signs?
- Whether this key child is able to talk about the different features of the surroundings, such as the sizes, shapes, uses and types of buildings or spaces they notice on a walk to the shops?
- Whether this key child can connect photographs to places in the environment and can work out a route, for example, from the local shop to their setting?
- How this key child talks about and evaluates the quality of their environment, for example, by talking about how the flower baskets improve the area and how the litter makes it look untidy?

Communities
- How this key child responds to a significant event, such as the birth of a baby or the death of a pet?
- The ways in which this key child recalls special events, such as weddings they attend?
- What interest this key child shows in stories, music and dance from a range of cultures?
- How this key child talks about the practices and beliefs of their friends?
- How this key child expresses their attitudes towards things, such as the differences in skin colours?
- How this key child responds to information about people's unfamiliar lifestyles?

Is there a particular aspect of this key child that you know less about?
How will you get this information? Through observations of the key child, talking to other staff or parents?

Knowledge and Understanding of the World

How do the adults support the development of Knowledge and Understanding of the World of their key children?

Think about all the children in your key group, and give yourself an overall score for each section on the scale below:

Exploration and Investigation
Do you?
- Encourage and respond to each child's signs of interest, and extend these through questions, discussions and further investigations?
- Give additional support to each child who is learning English as an additional language, through pictorial support, or familiar adults who can interpret for them?
- Help each child to notice and discuss patterns around them, for example, by taking rubbings from grates, covers or bricks?
- Encourage each child to raise questions and suggest solutions and answers?
- Examine change over time, for example, growing plants and then change that may be reversed, such as melting ice?

1	2	3	4	5

Just beginning to...   Doing it all!

Designing and Making
Do you?
- Introduce each child to appropriate tools for different materials?
- Provide a range of construction materials, including construction kits containing a variety of shapes, sizes and ways of joining, and support the children in their use?
- Discuss purposes of design and making tasks?
- Teach joining, measuring, cutting and finishing techniques and their names?
- Encourage each child's evaluations, helping them to use words to explain, such as 'longer', 'shorter', 'lighter'.

1	2	3	4	5

Just beginning to...   Doing it all!

ICT
Do you?
- Draw each child's attention to pieces of ICT apparatus they see or they use with adult supervision?
- Teach and encourage each child to click on different icons to cause things to happen in a computer program?
- Ensure safe use of all ICT apparatus and make appropriate risk assessments for their use?

1	2	3	4	5

Just beginning to...   Doing it all!

Time
Do you?
- Talk about and show interest in each child's lives and experiences?
- Use, and encourage each child to use the language of time in conversations, such as 'past', 'now' and 'then'.
- Encourage discussion of important events in the lives of people each child knows, such as their family.
- Make books of events, such as for the summer fair, building a climbing frame, a shopping expedition.
- Encourage role-play of events in each child's lives?
- Observe changes in the environment, such as through the seasons or as a building extension is completed?
- Sequence events, such as photographs of each child from birth?
- Use stories that introduce a sense of time and people from the past?
- Encourage each child to ask questions about events in each other's lives in discussions and explore these experiences in role-play?
- Compare artefacts of different times, for example, garden and household tools?
- Make the most of opportunities to value each child's histories and involve families in sharing the memories?

1	2	3	4	5

Just beginning to...   Doing it all!

continued on next sheet

How do the adults support the development of Knowledge and Understanding of the World of their key children? *(continued)*

Think about all the children in your key group, and give yourself an overall score for each section on the scale below:

Place
Do you?

● Create awareness of features of the environment in the setting and immediate local area by for example, going to the shops or a park?
● Introduce vocabulary to enable each child to talk about their observations and to ask questions?
● Encourage the parents to provide vocabulary in their home language to support language development and reinforce understanding?
● Use appropriate words, for example, 'town', 'village', 'road', 'temple' and 'synagogue' to help each child make distinctions in their observations?
● Help each child to find out about the environment by talking to people, examining photographs and simple maps and visiting local places?
● Encourage each child to express opinions on natural and built environments and give opportunities for them to hear different points of view on the quality of the environment?
● Ensure each child has opportunities to express themselves and learn the vocabulary to talk about their surroundings, drawing on and encouraging the home language to support the learning of English?
● Encourage the use of words that help each child to express opinions, such as 'busy', 'quiet' and 'pollution'?

1	2	3	4	5

Just beginning to...   Doing it all!

Communities
Do you?

● Introduce language that describes emotions, such as 'sad', 'happy', 'angry' and 'lonely', in conversations when each child expresses their feelings about special events?
● Use group times to share events in each child's lives?
● Listen carefully and ask questions that show respect for each child's individual contributions?
● Explain the significance of special events to the children?
● Visit workplaces and invite people who work in the community to talk to each child about their roles and wherever possible encourage the challenging of stereotypes by, for example, using a male midwife or a female fire-fighter?
● Introduce each child to a range of cultures and religions by, for example, telling stories, listening to music, dancing and eating foods from a range of cultures?
● Extend each child's knowledge of cultures within and beyond the setting?
● Ensure that any cultural assumptions and stereotypes that are already held are countered in activities?

1	2	3	4	5

Just beginning to...   Doing it all!

Who do you need to know more about?
Is there a particular aspect of the children's day and lives that you want to develop?

Knowledge and Understanding of the World

Resources and experiences that promote development of Knowledge and Understanding of the World.

Think about your environment. Do you have:

Exploration and Investigation
- Opportunities to use the local area for exploring both the built and the natural environment?
- Opportunities to observe things closely through a variety of means, including magnifiers and photographs?
- Opportunities to record findings by, for example, drawing, writing, making a model or photographing?
- A range of materials and objects to play with that work in different ways for different purposes, such as egg whisk, torch, other household implements, pulleys, construction kits and tape recorders?
- Opportunities to encourage the children to speculate on the reasons why things happen or how things work?

Designing and Making
- Ideas and stimuli for the children, such as photographs, books, visits and close observation of buildings?
- A range of tools such as scissors, hole punch, stapler, junior hacksaw, glue spreader, rolling pin and encourage the children to handle them carefully and use their correct names?
- Opportunities to make links with the children's experiences to provide opportunities to design and make things such as a ladder for Anansi the spider (in the West African traditional tale)?
- Opportunities for the children to practise skills, initiate and plan simple projects, and find their own solutions in the design and making process?
- Workshop areas that allow children real choices of techniques, materials and resources?

ICT
- Opportunities to ask the children to help press the button at the pelican crossing, or speak into an intercom?
- A range of programmable toys, as well as equipment involving ICT, such as computers?

Time
- Time when the children can discuss past events in their lives, such as what they did in the holidays?
- Photographs from home that show things such as a sunflower that their child took home from school in a pot, which has now grown taller than them?
- Full participation of the children learning English as an additional language by offering additional visual support and encouraging children to use their home language?
- Long-term growing projects, such as sowing seeds or looking after chicken eggs?
- Reference material for the children to use, such as old and recent photographs to compare?
- Projects about seasons using the local community as a resource?

Place
- Opportunities for visits to the local area?
- Play maps and small-world equipment for the children to create their own environments?
- Stories that help the children to make sense of different environments?
- Stimuli and resources for the children to create simple maps and plans, paintings, drawings and models of observations of known and imaginary landscapes?
- Opportunities to design practical, attractive environments, for example, taking care of the flowerbeds or organising equipment outdoors

Communities
- Opportunities to listen to the children wanting to talk about significant events and give them time to formulate thoughts and words to express feelings? Does this include providing the support of adults who share languages other than English with children?
- Ways of preserving memories of events, such as making a book, collecting photographs, tape-recording and so on.
- Opportunities for the children and families with experiences of living in different areas of the UK and other countries to bring in photographs and objects from their home cultures?
- Opportunities for the children to sample food from a variety of cultures, such as a Caribbean dish?
- Books that show a range of languages, dress and customs?
- Resources at circle time to enable the children to learn positive attitudes and behaviour towards people who are different to themselves?
- Modern photographs of parts of the world that are commonly stereotyped and misrepresented?

Rate your environment from 1–5

1	2	3	4	5

Just beginning to enable   Very enabling environment

How could you improve your environment and make it even more enabling for Knowledge and Understanding of the World?

Knowledge and Understanding of the World

Let's look at the Physical Development of your unique key children.

Read the following questions and think about each key child in your group as you read each one. Remember the many ways babies communicate and respond by eye contact, grasping, head-turning, wiggling toes, smiling, banging, vocalising and facial expressions.

How much do you know about _____ (key child's name)?

- How this baby moves around the space on their feet, bottom, back, tummy, hands and knees?

- How this baby uses their senses to explore the environment?

- What kind of movements this baby is likely to make, such as pulling to stand, walking?

- What this baby does when they are hungry or thirsty?

- What are this baby's hunger patterns?

- How this baby shows they are relaxed when they feel safe and cared for?

- How this baby's behaviour changes as they get tired and need sleep?

- How this baby shows that they need help?

- What this baby likes to reach for and play with, grasp and clutch at, such as toes, toys, sand and paint?

- What are the actions this baby makes, for example, clapping, pointing, grasping and dropping things?

- What sensory experiences this baby enjoys?

- What patterns of behaviour (schemas) this baby is showing, such as transporting objects, enveloping, circling?

Is there a particular aspect of this baby that you know less about?

How will you get this information? Through observations of the baby, talking to other staff or parents?

Physical Development

How do the adults support the Physical Development of their key children?

Think about all the babies in your key group, and give yourself an overall score for each section on the scale below:

Do you?

- Let each baby kick and stretch freely on their tummies and backs?
- Encourage each baby to explore the space near them by putting interesting things beside them, for example, crinkly paper, light material?
- Give each baby varied physical experiences, such as bouncing, rolling and rocking, indoors and outdoors?
- Encourage each baby to play with things they can grasp, squeeze and throw safely?
- Encourage each baby to notice the other babies and children as they come near to them?
- Encourage and support each baby to stand and walk as they develop these skills?
- Encourage each baby to play games with each other, for example, rolling, throwing, fetching and receiving games when they are able to?
- Talk to and pat each baby gently to remind them that you are there and keeping them safe?
- Help each baby enjoy their food and try healthy choices by combining favourites with new tastes and textures?
- Have space for each baby to move in, ensuring they are safe but not restricting their exploring?
- Keep aware that each baby has little sense of danger when they are focused on getting something they want?
- Play games with each baby, for example, offering toys, imitating the babies play?
- Encourage each baby to gradually share control of the bottle with you?
- Use feeding, changing and bathing times as opportunities to play finger rhymes, such as 'Round and round the garden'?
- Show each baby how to make marks in dough or paint alongside them?

1	2	3	4	5

Just beginning to...   Doing it all!

Do you discuss with parents (using support/translation as needed):

- Their baby's feeding patterns, such as when and how they sit?
- The foods and drinks the baby has at home?
- The cultural needs and expectations for skin and hair care so that all the babies' needs are met appropriately and those parents' wishes are respected?

1	2	3	4	5

Just beginning to...   Doing it all!

Who do you need to know more about?

Is there a particular aspect of the babies' day and lives that you want to develop?

Physical Development

Resources and experiences that promote Physical Development.

Think about your environment. Do you have:

- Resources such as beanbags, cones, balls and hoops that encourage the babies to move around?

- Baby massage sessions to help the babies feel nurtured and have a positive sense of well-being?

- Comfortable, accessible places where babies can rest or sleep when they want to?

- Alternative activities for babies who do not want to sleep at the same time as others?

- An environment where the babies can move freely but safely?

- Well-planned safe areas with plenty of space for the babies to move, roll, stretch and explore in, indoors and outdoors?

- Resources that move or make a noise when touched to encourage the babies to reach out their arms and legs?

- Novelty in the environment that encourages the babies to use all their senses and move around indoors and outdoors?

- Low-level equipment so that babies can pull up to standing and equipment positioned so that the babies can cruise?

- Tunnels, slopes and low level steps to challenge the babies?

- Accessible toys that the babies can reach and fetch?

- Space to encourage free movement for the babies?

- Baskets of toys for babies to play with while waiting to be fed, or in the pram?

- Objects to be sucked, pulled, squeezed and held to develop fine motor skills?

- Resources that stimulate the babies to handle and manipulate things, for example, toys with buttons to press, books with flaps?

- Gloop and other materials that babies can make marks in by putting their fingers in and out of the materials?

Rate your environment from 1–5

1	2	3	4	5

Just beginning to enable   Very enabling environment

How could you improve your environment and make it even more enabling for Physical Development?

Physical Development

Let's look at the Physical Development of your unique key children.

Read the following questions and think about each key child in your group as you read each one. Remember the many ways babies communicate and respond by eye contact, grasping, head-turning, wiggling toes, smiling, banging, vocalising and facial expressions.

How much do you know about _____ **(key child's name)?**

Movement and Space

- How this key child moves their body to show how they feel when excited, interested, annoyed or happy?
- What sensory experiences this key child enjoys, such as rolling, rocking, spinning and physical contact with adults?
- What physical skills this key child is developing, such as creeping, crawling, climbing, walking, throwing?
- What physical skills this key child can achieve, for example, jumping with two feet, kicking a ball, balancing on one leg?
- How this key child will experiment with movement, for example, balancing, turning upside down, crawling and rolling?
- How this key child responds physically to stimuli such as seeing an aeroplane overhead?
- How this key child responds to music?
- How this key child joins movements, such as stopping and jumping, climbing and turning?
- How this key child uses their body to express themselves imaginatively?

Health and Bodily Awareness

- How much this key child is aware of bladder and bowel urges?
- What this key child likes and dislikes in food, drink and activity?
- What patterns of play, such as climbing on and off a step, this child enjoys?
- How this key child communicates their need for drink, food or to show they need changing?

Using Equipment and Materials

- How this key child prefers to eat their food, for example, with fingers, a fork or spoon?
- How this key child is able to use objects conventionally, such as recognise that you drink from a cup?
- How this key child is developing fine movement of their fingers and hands to grip, twist, bang and make marks, such as balance blocks to make a structure?
- How this key child shows increasing control of equipment and materials, for example, in banging hammers, holding beaters, turning pages of a book?

Is there a particular aspect of this key child that you know less about?

How will you get this information? Through observations of the key child, talking to other staff or parents?

Physical Development

How do the adults support the Physical Development of their key children?

Think about all the children in your key group, and give yourself an overall score for each section on the scale below:

Do you?

- Encourage each child to independently explore patterns of behaviour (schemas), for example, transporting, throwing, enveloping, circling and so on?
- Use music so each child can explore rhythm and movement?
- Ensure you have clear, suitable space for each child's rapid and sometimes unpredictable movements?
- Understand that each child can be very energetic for short bursts and needs time to relax and rest throughout the day?
- Encourage each child to persevere at a skill?
- Value the different ways each child may choose to move?
- Give as much opportunity for each child to move freely between indoors and outdoors?
- Talk to each child about exploring different ways of moving, for example, slithering, squirming, twisting like a snake?
- Encourage each child to move using different body parts, such as tiptoe?
- Encourage each child to move at different speeds, for example, fast, slow?
- Encourage different body tension activities, such as stretching, reaching, curling and so on?
- Know when each child may overstretch themselves and keep them safe?
- Introduce spatial language, for example, between, through, above and so on?
- Have flexible toileting routines to encourage independence?
- Value each child's choices and encourage them to try something new and healthy?
- Involve each child in preparing food?
- Encourage repetition in movement and sensory experiences?
- Encourage each child to talk about what they like to eat, while reinforcing messages about healthy eating?
- Help each child develop a sense of danger in their play indoors and out?
- Have mealtimes that encourage each child to independently eat and drink?
- Help each child find comfortable ways to grasp and hold things, for example, paintbrushes, teapot in role-play?
- Encourage each child to be independent, for example, in pouring drinks, putting on coats?

1	2	3	4	5

Just beginning to...   Doing it all!

Do you discuss with parents (using support/translation as needed):

- Their child's toileting routine at home?
- The cultural expectations for toileting, such as whether boys sit or stand?
- How children eat and drink at home, for example, the use of hands?

1	2	3	4	5

Just beginning to...   Doing it all!

Who do you need to know more about?

Is there a particular aspect of the children's day and lives that you want to develop?

Physical Development

Resources and experiences that promote Physical Development.

Think about your environment. Do you have:

- Equipment for the children who are physically disabled that is easily accessible and meets their individual needs?

- Stories that encourage different ways of moving, for example, *We're Going on a Bear Hunt*, Michael Rosen (Walker Books Ltd)?

- Play equipment and soft play materials that encourage crawling, rolling, climbing and tumbling?

- Large play equipment that can be used in different ways, for example, boxes, ladders, barrels, 'A' frames?

- Time for free physical play and planned activities that encourage the children to practise and experiment their physical skills?

- Risk assessments and safe spaces where the children can move safely and freely?

- Real and role-play opportunities to create pathways, for example, making road layouts, taking the pushchair to the home corner?

- CDs and tape players, scarves, streamers and musical instruments so that children can respond spontaneously to music?

- Activities that involve moving and stopping, for example, musical bumps?

- Choices for the children for toileting, such as potties, trainer seats or steps?

- Routines that enable the children to look after themselves, for example, putting their clothes and aprons on hooks, washing themselves?

- Time to discuss healthy options, such as drinking water, milk or juice?

- Strategies to keep children safe while not inhibiting risk-taking?

- A colourful daily menu displaying healthy meals and snacks encouraging the children to try new things?

Rate your environment from 1–5

1	2	3	4	5

Just beginning to enable   Very enabling environment

How could you improve your environment and make it even more enabling for Physical Development?

Physical Development

Let's look at the Physical Development of your unique key children.

Read the following questions and think about each key child in your group as you read each one.

How much do you know about _____ (key child's name)?

Movement and Space

- What physical activities this key child enjoys and can do confidently?
- How well this key child manages space and avoiding banging into other children or objects with their body or toys?
- What physical skills this key child could move on to as a new challenge?
- What physical activity this key child perseveres at?
- The ideas this key child suggests to make things fair?
- How much this key child can manage to and understand the need to stay safe physically?
- How developed this key child's fine motor skills are, for example, using a brush or pen?
- How well this key child can balance and climb?
- How coordinated this key child is with movement?

Health and Bodily Awareness

- How much this key child recognises and understands their needs, such as asking for help with a shoe lace when it is undone?
- When this key child demonstrates understanding of the importance of healthy practices, such as asking for a tissue to blow their nose, or putting a cup in the sink to be washed?
- How much this key child understands the need for a rest or a drink after activity?
- What this key child understands of about how to maintain good health, for example, having teeth checked at the dentist?
- This key child's ability to understand what happens to their body after exercise?

Using Equipment and Materials

- What inspires this key child to create or construct?
- This key child's hand-eye coordination in picking up small objects, threading, posting?
- How well this key child fastens and unfastens items, such as containers, clothes, cupboards?
- How safely and appropriately this key child can use materials and equipment?
- This key child's preferred hand for putting on clothes or using a brush?
- What ball skills this key child has, such as kicking, throwing and catching?
- What malleable materials this child likes to play with?
- How this key child independently demonstrates their understanding of the need to handle equipment safely, such as carrying a chair correctly?
- What large play equipment this child likes to play with, such as climbing frames?

Is there a particular aspect of this key child that you know less about?

How will you get this information? Through observations of the key child, talking to other staff or parents?

Physical Development

How do the adults support the Physical Development of their key children?

Think about all the children in your key group, and give yourself an overall score for each section on the scale below:

Movement and Space
Do you?
- Teach skills to each child to help keep them safe?
- Encourage each child to move with controlled effort, for example, to be floppy, heavy, gentle, reach and stretch?
- Use music to create moods, such as sad, cross, happy, and talk about how people express their moods in movement?
- Lead imaginative movement sessions based on each child's current interests, for example, shadows?
- Encourage and motivate each child to be active and energetic through games like Follow the Leader and other lively games?
- Talk about why each child needs to take care when moving around?
- Have some simple rules for movement to remind them how to move with hurting themselves or others?
- Praise each child when they consider other children or collaborate in tasks?
- Encourage each child to persevere and not give up by praising or guiding?
- Encourage each child to use a variety of vocabulary to describe movement, such as gallop, slither?
- Help each child to communicate and express their imaginative ideas through their bodies?
- Teach each child the vocabulary associated with body parts and bodily activity?
- Help each child think about how their movement and actions can impact on others?
- Pose physical challenges for each child?
- Review the equipment and space available to meet each child's needs?

1	2	3	4	5

Just beginning to...   Doing it all!

Health and Bodily Awareness
Do you?
- Talk to each child about their need to rest, sleep, eat, drink and hygiene to help them recognise their own needs?
- Have opportunities for each child to become more independent in hand-washing, getting tissues and so on?
- Support each child in making healthy choices about the food they eat?
- Encourage each child to notice the change in their bodies after being active?
- Promote an awareness of the importance of exercise and why it is part of being healthy?
- Have an awareness of the health needs of each child, for example, allergies?
- Remain sensitive that families may not have healthy patterns at home while you are encouraging this at the setting?
- Find ways of being active that match each child's interests, needs and abilities?
- Discuss with each child the effect of the environment and ways to manage this, for example, opening a window to stay cool?

1	2	3	4	5

Just beginning to...   Doing it all!

Using Equipment and Materials
Do you?
- Teach each child the skills they need to use equipment safely, such as scissors and other tools?
- Give each child a chance to practise these skills?
- Check each child's clothes for safety, for example, checking coat zips can't get tangled in bike wheels?
- Introduce the vocabulary of direction, for example, 'up', 'down', 'clockwise', 'anticlockwise'?
- Encourage each child's large arm and hand movements to strengthen their hands and fingers, for example, throwing, catching?
- Use a range of language for manipulating materials, for example, 'squeeze', 'prod', and to describe materials, such as 'spiky', 'smooth'?
- Explain why safety is important in handling tools, equipment and materials?
- Have sensible rules for everyone to follow when using equipment and materials?
- Talk to each child about what they are doing, their plans and what they would do differently next time?

1	2	3	4	5

Just beginning to...   Doing it all!

Physical Development

Resources and experiences that promote Physical Development.

Think about your environment. Do you have:

Movement and Space

- Floor coverings and spaces that allow the children to tackle different levels, for example, tunnels, mats, benches and surfaces such as hilly, flat, grass, pebbles, asphalt, smooth floors, carpet?
- Appropriate equipment for the size and weight of the children in the group?
- Activities that allow moving in different ways and at different speeds?
- Resources to promote balancing, for example, lines to balance on?
- Boundaries for different types of physical activities, for example, for wheeled toys or balls?
- Rules for use of these spaces?
- Sufficient equipment so the children don't have to wait a long time for their turn?
- Construction materials and other open-ended resources such as crates, blocks and boxes for large-scale building, to make dens or personal spaces?
- Large portable equipment that the children can move around safely and cooperatively to make structures?
- Photographs to put in a book about 'Me and the things I can do'?
- Resources for target throwing, rolling, catching and kicking?
- A collection of rhymes to teach body parts, including, for example, 'Head, shoulders, knees and toes'?
- Time and space to play energetically daily indoors or outdoors?
- Regular risk assessments and checks of resources, for example, clean fabric, planks free from splinters?
- Imaginative, active, physical experiences, such as going on a bear hunt?

Health and Bodily Awareness

- A cosy place with cushions for the children to rest quietly as needed?
- Daily activities that help keep all the children active including wheelchair users?
- Time for the children to recover when out of breath?
- Water containers which the children can use easily and get a drink as needed?

Using Equipment and Materials

- A range of accessible and available equipment for all the children for all of the day or session as far as possible?
- Activities that promote the use of manipulative skills, for example, cooking, painting?
- Activities that use the whole hand, such as finger painting or one finger, such as in the sand?
- Left-handed tools, especially scissors for left-handed children?
- A wide range of materials to encourage manipulation, for example, clay, play dough, small-world toys, threading, posting?
- A choice of tools or materials to achieve the desired effect?
- Tweezers, tongs and small scoops for use in sand and investigation?
- A range of construction toys of different sizes and materials that fix together in a variety of ways, such as twisting, slotting, magnetism, pushing?

Rate your environment from 1–5

1	2	3	4	5

Just beginning to enable   Very enabling environment

How could you improve your environment and make it even more enabling for Physical Development?

Physical Development

Let's look at the Creative Development of your unique key children.

Read the following questions and think about each key child in your group as you read each one. Remember the many ways babies communicate and respond, by eye-contact, grasping, head-turning, wiggling toes, smiling, banging, vocalising and facial expressions.

How much do you know about _____ **(key child's name)?**

- How this baby shows emotion through the movements of fingers, arms and bodies?

- What this baby's favourite materials, music, lights and aromas are?

- How this baby responds when they touch or feel something such as warm milk or a fluffy toy?

- What this baby likes to make marks in and the tools they like to use to make them?

- How this baby moves their whole body as they explore media?

- How this baby responds to voices, sounds and music, such as lullabies?

- The different ways this baby moves in response to sounds, for example, patting the floor when on their tummy, flexing and relaxing legs or opening and closing their palms?

- What this baby smiles with pleasure at when playing with recognisable playthings?

- How this baby joins in with you, moving their head or making sounds as you say, for example, 'The dog went woof, woof'.

Is there a particular aspect of this baby that you know less about?

How will you get this information? Through observations of the baby, talking to other staff or parents?

Creative Development

The EYFS: Am I getting it right? © Anita Soni & Sue Bristow

How do the adults support the Creative Development of their key children?

Think about all the children in your key group, and give yourself an overall score for each section on the scale below:

Do you?

- Use gentle touch to trace 'Round and Round the Garden' or to pat hands for 'Pat-a-Cake' with the babies?

- Maintain a calm atmosphere of a light room or area by playing quiet music so that the babies can rest from stimulation for short periods?

- Talk to the babies about the sensations of different materials they feel, whether they are cold or warm, smooth or soft?

- Encourage the babies to make marks and to squeeze and feel media such as paint, gloop, dough and bubbles?

- Sing action rhymes such as 'Head, Shoulders, Knees and Toes' or clap and sing about something you are doing such as 'We're getting Mina ready for bed'?

- Imitate familiar sounds such as 'quack, quack', encouraging the babies to join in?

- Play games such as hiding the snake behind your back and slowly showing it coming round the corner of the play mat?

- Make exaggerated facial movements when you tell a story or join in pretend play, so that the babies notice changes in your body language?

1	2	3	4	5

Just beginning to...   Doing it all!

Do you discuss with parents (using support/translation as needed):

- What songs and action rhymes they sing at home?

1	2	3	4	5

Just beginning to...   Doing it all!

Who do you need to know more about?

Is there a particular aspect of the babies' day and lives that you want to develop?

Resources and experiences that promote Creative Development.

Think about your environment. Do you have:

- Sensory resources such as soft feathers, silk squares and pom-poms available to the babies and vary the experiences over time?

- A basket of things that each baby likes to explore?

- Big sheets of plastic or paper on the floor so that the babies can be near or crawl on to it to make marks or add materials using large motor movements, such as sprinkling, throwing or spreading paint, glue, torn paper or other materials?

- A variety of toys that will make different sounds so that you can talk about the sounds the babies hear when they mouth or hold?

- A range of puppets that glide along the table, or dance around on the end of a fist in time to some lively music?

- A variety of familiar toys and playthings that the babies enjoy looking at, listening to, touching, grasping and squeezing?

- Exaggerated facial gestures and expressions when you play pretend games?

Rate your environment from 1–5

1	2	3	4	5

Just beginning to enable   Very enabling environment

How could you improve your environment and make it even more enabling for Creative Development?

Creative Development

Let's look at the Creative Development of your unique key children.

Read the following questions and think about each key child in your group as you read each one.

How much do you know about _____ (key child's name)?

Being Creative – Responding to Experiences, Expressing and Communicating Ideas

● The ways that this key child may repeat actions or make tuneful sounds as they climb steps, or step up and down from a stool?

● What this key child does in response to their experiences such as word plays, using signs, body language or gestures?

Exploring Media and Materials

● The processes this key child engages in as they explore and experiment with media?

● The inventive ways in which this key child adds, or mixes media, or wallows in particular experiences?

Creating Music and Dance

● How this key child likes to use shakers, blocks and body movements when they hear music, or to explore sound?

● How this key child responds to different songs, dance or music?

Developing Imagination and Imaginative Play

● How this key child may turn to pretend play when an object comes to hand, for example, when a child uses a wooden block as a telephone?

● This key child's make-believe play?

Is there a particular aspect of this key child that you know less about?

How will you get this information? Through observations of the key child, talking to other staff or parents?

Creative Development

How do the adults support the Creative Development of their key children?

Think about all the children in your key group, and give yourself an overall score for each section on the scale below:

Do you?

- Support each child's patterns of play in different activities, for example, transporting blocks into the sand tray?
- Help each child to value their creative responses by showing interest in the way they move, represent or express their mood?
- Accept wholeheartedly each child's creations and help them to see them as something unique and valuable?
- Show interest in each child's creative processes and talk to them about what they mean to them?
- Listen with each child to a variety of sounds, talking about their favourite sounds, songs and music?
- Introduce each child to language to describe sounds and rhythm, such as loud and soft, fast and slow?
- Help each child to listen to music and watch dance when opportunities arise, encouraging them to focus on how sound and movement develops from feelings and ideas?
- Show genuine interest and be willing to play along with each child who is beginning to pretend?
- Sometimes speak quietly, slowly or gruffly for fun in pretend scenarios with each child?

1	2	3	4	5

Just beginning to...   Doing it all!

Do you discuss with parents (using support/translation as needed):

- How they respond to their child's creative responses?
- What their child's patterns of play are?

1	2	3	4	5

Just beginning to...   Doing it all!

Who do you need to know more about?

Is there a particular aspect of the children's day and lives that you want to develop?

The EYFS: Am I getting it right? © Anita Soni & Sue Bristow

Resources and experiences that promote Creative Development.

Think about your environment. Do you have:

- Props such as streamers for the children to wave to make swirling lines, or place shiny mobiles made from unwanted CDs, in the trees to whirl in the wind?

- Enough time for the children to express their thoughts, ideas and feelings in a variety of ways, such as in role-play, by painting and by responding to music?

- Notes detailing the processes involved in a child's creations, to share with parents?

- Unusual or interesting materials and resources that inspire exploration such as textured wall covering, translucent paper and so on?

- A sound line using a variety of objects strung safely that will make different sounds, such as wood, pans and plastic bottles filled with different things?

- Dancers and musicians from theatre groups, the locality or a nearby school so that the children can begin to experience live performances?

- A wide range of musicians and storytellers from a variety of cultural backgrounds to extend children's experiences and to reflect their cultural heritages?

- A variety of familiar resources reflecting everyday life, such as magazines, fabric shopping bags, telephones or washing materials?

- Additional resources reflecting interests such as tunics, cloaks and bags?

Rate your environment from 1–5

1	2	3	4	5

Just beginning to enable   Very enabling environment

How could you improve your environment and make it even more enabling for Creative Development?

Creative Development

Let's look at the Creative Development of your unique key children.

Read the following questions and think about each key child in your group as you read each one.

How much do you know about _____ (key child's name)?

Being Creative – Responding to Experiences, Expressing and Communicating Ideas

- How does this key child capture their experiences, for example, by finding materials to make wings from a large piece of red paper after watching some ladybirds in the garden?
- How does this key child explore materials and the effects they can create, such as making swirling lines with scarves and streamers by twirling them around?
- What connections this key child makes as they respond to different experiences, for example, remembering being cold at Diwali and seeing the cheery lights may inspire one child to begin to dance like the flames of the Diwali lamps.
- How this key child responds to new experiences and how they respond differently to similar experiences, for example, a child may run around moving their arms rhythmically when they see or hear a train, while another day they may want to draw or paint a train.
- How this key child designs and creates, either using their own ideas or developing those of others?

Exploring Media and Materials

- How this key child responds to different textures, for example, touching sections of a texture display with their fingers, or feeling it with their cheek to get a sense of different the properties?
- Whether this key child is beginning to notice differences between colours?
- Whether this key child spontaneously makes marks and movements on paper or whether they imitate the movements and marks of others?
- Whether this key child is beginning to describe the objects they represent?
- What patterns and structures this key child talks about, makes or constructs?
- What inventive ways this key child mixes colours?
- What decisions this key child makes about colour choices?
- How this key child experiments to create new effects and textures, for example, by drizzling glue over wool, or squirting pools of colour on to paper?
- How this key child combines their creative skills and imagination to create something new, for example, when a small group of children are using large blocks to represent their experience of a visit to the ferry port. After much discussion and negotiation they make arrows for the one-way system and a variety of signs and symbols. They tell the stories of people who will go to the ferry and wonder about whether one family will get there on time.
- What ways this key child creates and constructs, and how their explorations lead to new understanding about media?

Creating Music and Dance

- What ways this key child chooses to explore sound, song or movement, for example, a group of children explore a rainforest theme through music and movement. Some use instruments to make the sounds of the rainforest, while others imitate the movements of the rainforest animals.
- What this key child's interest is in exploring sound, rhythm and the arts, for example, in response to listening to music that represents the sea, the children compose their own sound picture. This leads them to planning and constructing a pirate ship in the role-play area and using materials in the art and technology area to make hats, flags and other props to support play.

Developing Imagination and Imaginative Play

- What range of experiences this key child represents through imaginative play?
- How this key child responds in different ways to stories, ideas and their own life experiences?
- What ways stories are developed in this key child's play, for example, children may start 'swimming' on the 'beach' and extend their storyline into meeting with a mermaid and their adventures with her.

Is there a particular aspect of this key child that you know less about?
How will you get this information? Through observations of the key child, talking to other staff or parents?

Creative Development

How do the adults support the Creative Development of their key children?

Think about all the children in your key group, and give yourself an overall score for each section on the scale below:

Being Creative – Responding to Experiences, Expressing and Communicating Ideas
Do you?
- Provide appropriate materials and extend each child's thinking through involvement in their play, using questions thoughtfully and appropriately?
- Encourage each child to describe experiences?
- Show interest in each child's responses, observing their actions and listening carefully?
- Support each child in expressing opinions and introduce language such as 'like', 'dislike', 'prefer' and 'disagree'?
- Respond to each child's changing interests and the way they respond to experiences differently when they are in a happy, sad or reflective mood?

1	2	3	4	5

Just beginning to...   Doing it all!

Exploring Media and Materials
Do you?
- Make time and space for each child to express their curiosity and explore the environment using all of their senses?
- Talk to each child about images or effects that they see, such as the effect of light hitting a shiny piece of paper?
- Demonstrate and teach skills and techniques associated with the things each child is doing, for example, show them how to stop the paint from dripping or how to balance bricks so that they do not fall down?
- Introduce each child to a wide range of music, painting and sculpture?
- Encourage each child to take time to think about painting or sculpture that is unfamiliar to them before they talk about it or express an opinion?
- Make suggestions and ask questions to extend each child's ideas of what is possible, for example, 'I wonder what would happen if...'?
- Support each child in thinking about what they make, the processes that may be involved and the materials and resources they might need, for example, a photograph to remind them what the climbing frame is like
- Talk to each child about ways of finding out what they can do with different media and what happens when they put different things together such as sand, paint and sawdust?
- Help each child to develop a problem solving approach to overcome hindrances as they explore possibilities that media combinations present. Offer advice and additional resources as appropriate?
- Alert each child to changes in properties of media as they are transformed through becoming wet, dry, flaky or fixed. Talk about what is happening, helping them to think about cause and effect?

1	2	3	4	5

Just beginning to...   Doing it all!

Creating Music and Dance
Do you?
- Widen each child's experience of music from different cultures, through experiences with different instruments and styles so that they are inspired to experiment, imitate, enjoy and extend their own expressions?
- Support each child's developing understanding of the ways in which paintings, pictures and music and dance can express different ideas, thoughts and feelings?
- Encourage discussion about the beauty of nature and people's responsibility to care for it? Help each child to support other children and offer another viewpoint?

1	2	3	4	5

Just beginning to...   Doing it all!

Developing Imagination and Imaginative Play
Do you?
- Support each child's excursions into imaginary worlds by encouraging inventiveness, offering support and advice on occasions and ensuring that they have experiences that stimulate their interest?
- Tell stories based on each child's experiences and the people and places they know well?
- Carefully support the children who are less confident?
- Introduce descriptive language to support each child, for example, 'rustle' and 'shuffle'?

1	2	3	4	5

Just beginning to...   Doing it all!

Who do you need to know more about?
Is there a particular aspect of the children's day and lives that you want to develop?

Creative Development

Resources and experiences that promote Creative Development.

Think about your environment. Do you have:

Being Creative – Responding to Experiences, Expressing and Communicating Ideas

- Time for the children to express their thoughts, ideas and feelings in a variety of ways, for example, in role-play, by painting and by responding to music?
- Opportunities to discuss and appreciate the beauty around them in nature and the environment?
- Opportunities to introduce language that enables the children to talk about their experiences in greater depth and detail?
- Examples of how other people have responded to experiences to talk about with the children to help them make links and connections?
- An area for resources and materials so that the children can make their own choices in order to express their ideas?
- Sensitivity to the needs of children who may not be able to express themselves easily in English, using interpreter support from known adults, or strategies such as picture cards to enable children to express preferences?

Exploring Media and Materials

- Opportunities to introduce vocabulary to enable the children to talk about their observations and experiences, for example, 'smooth', 'rough', 'prickly', 'flat' and so on.
- A wide range of materials, resources and sensory experiences to enable children to explore colour, texture and space?
- Opportunities to document the processes children go through to create their own 'work'?
- A place where work in progress can be kept safely?
- Opportunities to talk to the children about where they can see models and plans in the environment, for example, at the local planning office, in the town square, or at the new apartments down the road?

Creating Media and Dance

- Experiences that involve all the senses and movement?
- Opportunities to extend the children's experience and expand their imagination through the provision of pictures, painting, poems, music, dance and story?
- A stimulus for imaginative recreation and composition by introducing atmospheric features in the role-play area, such as the sounds of rain beating on a roof, or placing a spotlight to suggest a stage set?

Developing Imagination and Imaginative Play

- Opportunities for offering story stimulus by suggesting an imaginary event or set of circumstances, such as, 'This bear has arrived in the post. He has a letter pinned to his jacket. It says "Please look after this bear". We should look after him in our room. How can we do that?'.
- Accessible materials so that children are able to imagine and bring to fruition their projects and ideas while they are still fresh in their minds and important to them?
- Opportunities indoors and outdoors to support the different interests of children, for example, in role-play of a builder's yard, encourage narratives to do with building and mending?
- Props for telling stories that support children to tell stories about their own experiences and others?

Rate your environment from 1–5

1	2	3	4	5

Just beginning to enable   Very enabling environment

How could you improve your environment and make it even more enabling for Creative Development?

Creative Development